An Elementary Study of Insects

Leonard Haseman

CONTENTS.

(3) Breeding work.

CHAPTER VII THE APPLE WORM:

(1) Brief discussion of the different stages of the pest, its work and remedies for its control.
(2) Observations and breeding work.

CHAPTER VIII THE TOMATO OR TOBACCO WORM:

(1) Brief discussion of stages, work and habits.
(2) Study and observation.

CHAPTER IX THE FIREFLY:

(1) Brief discussion of the insect.
(2) Observations and studies.

CHAPTER X THE WHITE GRUB OR JUNE-BUG:

(1) Discussion of the insect as a pest and its habits and stages.
(2) Observations and studies.

CHAPTER XI THE COLORADO POTATO BEETLE:

(1) Brief discussion of the pest.
(2) Observations and studies.

CHAPTER XII THE LADY-BEETLE:

(1) Brief discussion of habits and appearance of the lady-beetles, and their value as friends.
(2) Observations and studies.

CHAPTER XIII THE DRAGON-FLY:

(1) Discussion of life and habits of insect.
(2) Observations and field studies.

CHAPTER XIV THE SQUASH BUG:

(1) Discussion of habits, injury and control of pest.
(2) Observations and field studies.

CHAPTER XV THE PLANT-LOUSE:

(1) Discussion of habits, injury and control of pest.
(2) Observations and field studies.

INTRODUCTION

In the preparation of a book of this nature, to be used in the grade schools, we realize that the one fundamental thing to keep in mind is the economic importance of the insect, be it good or bad. The child wants to know what is good and what is bad and how he can make use of the good and how he can get rid of the bad. And yet there is something more associated with the life, work and development of each tiny insect. There is a story—a story of growth, not unlike that of the developing child, a story of courage, strife and ultimate success or failure, which is as interesting and of greater value to the child than many of the stories of adventure and of historical facts. Snatches of these stories will appear in the following chapters along with the studies on insects and their economic importance.

In the development of our grade school system, especially in the rural districts, there is a growing demand for some practical work along with the regular cultural studies. To the child in the rural schools, practical knowledge naturally tends toward agriculture. Many of these boys and girls do not have a chance to pursue studies beyond the grades and it therefore becomes necessary to introduce some elementary agriculture into the grades to supply the natural craving of this vast assemblage of children in the rural schools of our land.

In the search for a study which will give unlimited scope for independent thought and observation and which will lead the child to understand better the forces of nature that affect agriculture, nothing is so readily available and attractive to the child as nature study, an elementary study of the natural sciences. In fact agriculture is primarily a course in nature study where we study how plants and animals struggle for existence.

There is a period in the life of every child when he is especially susceptible to the "call of the fields;" when he roams through woods or by shady brooks gathering flowers, fishing for mud-cats and cleaning out bumble-bees' nests. It is often compared with the life of the savage and is merely the outward expression of an inward craving for a closer relation with nature and her creatures. If one can reach a child while at that age he has a ready listener and an apt pupil. That is the time to guide and instruct the child along the line of nature study.

The most important questions confronting the average teacher in the grade schools are: "What material shall I use and how shall I proceed to direct the child along this line?" First of all use that material which is most readily available, which is most familiar to the child and which will attract and hold his attention. There is nothing so readily available and so generally interesting to both boys and girls as are the thousands of fluttering, buzzing, hopping and creeping forms of insects. They are present everywhere, in all seasons and are known to every child of the city or farm. They are easily observed in the field and can be kept in confinement for study. Many of them are of the greatest importance to man; a study of them becomes of special value.

In pursuing a study of nature and her creatures one should go into the woods and fields as much as possible and study them where they are found. In this way one can determine how they live together, what they feed on and the various other questions which the inquisitive mind of a healthy child will ask. When field work is not possible, gather the insects and keep them alive in jars where they can be fed and observed. Some forms cannot be kept in confinement and in such cases samples should be killed and pinned, thereby forming a collection for study.

Most of the forms which are included in the following chapters can be kept in confinement in glass jars or studies out doors. The studies have been made so general that in case the particular form mentioned is not available any closely related form can be used. Each child should make a small collection of living and pinned insects for study and should be encouraged to observe insects and their work in the field. The collections and many of the observations could be made to good advantage during the summer vacation when the insects are most abundant and active.

Pupils should not be encouraged merely to make observations, but they should be required to record them as well. Brief descriptions of the appearance and development of insects, the injury they do, and remedies for the same, will help fix in mind facts which otherwise might soon be forgotten. Drawings, whenever possible, should also be required. The pupil who can record observations accurately with drawings will not soon forget them. The teacher should therefore require each pupil to provide himself with a note-book for keeping brief, but accurate notes and careful drawings. The drawings should be made with a hard lead pencil on un-ruled paper, the size of the note-book, and the pupils should be encouraged to be neat and accurate.

The author wishes to take this opportunity of expressing his deep appreciation for the many helpful suggestions and other assistance which Mr. R. H. Emberson, superintendent of Boys and Girls Club Work in Missouri, has given. It was his life-long devotion to the boys and girls of the grade schools and his keen appreciation of their needs that lead him first to suggest to the author the importance of preparing this little book for their use.

LEONARD HASEMAN

University of Missouri.

"The study of entomology is one of the most fascinating of pursuits. It takes its votaries into the treasure-houses of Nature, and explains some of the wonderful series of links which form the great chain of creation. It lays open before us another world, of which we have been hitherto unconscious, and shows us that the tiniest insect, so small perhaps that the unaided eye can scarcely see it, has its work to do in the world, and does it."

—REV. J. G. WOOD.

CHAPTER I

INSECTS

"There is a difference between a grub and a butterfly; yet your butterfly was a grub."

—SHAKESPEARE.

IN undertaking a study of insects it is well first of all to know something about what they are, their general nature, appearance, habits and development. The insects comprise the largest group of animals on the globe. There are about four times as many different kinds of insects as all other kinds of animals combined. Insects vary greatly in size. Some are as large as small birds, while others are so small that a thousand placed in one pile would not equal the size of a pea.

Insects are commonly spoken of as "bugs." This term, however, is properly used only when referring to the one order of insects which includes the sap and blood-sucking insects such as the chinch bug, bed-bug, squash bug, and the like. Then too, there are many so-called "bugs" which are not insects at all. Spiders, thousand-legs, crawfishes and even earth-worms are often spoken of as bugs.

What They Are

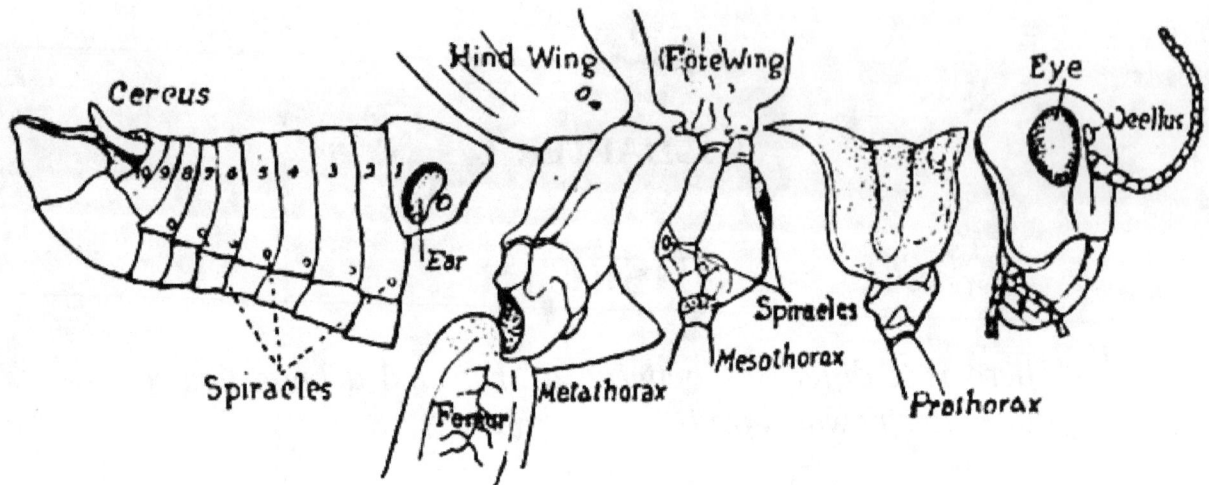

Side view of grasshopper with wings and legs partly removed. Note the division of the body into head, thorax, composed of prothorax, mesothorax and metathorax, and abdomen consisting of ring-like segments.

Insects are variously formed, but as a rule the mature ones have three and only three pairs of legs, one pair of feelers, one pair of large eyes, and one or two pairs of wings. The body is divided into a head, thorax and abdomen. The head bears the eyes, feelers and mouth, the thorax bears the legs and wings, and the abdomen is made up of a number of segments. The presence of wings at once decides whether or not it is an insect, for, aside from bats and birds, insects alone have true wings. These are the distinguishing characters of the full grown insect, but, like birds, they hatch from eggs and while young do not always look like their parents. When young they may take on various shapes as caterpillars, borers, maggots, grubs, hoppers, and the like. Young insects are often difficult to distinguish from true worms, centipedes, snails, and such forms, but after one has collected and reared some of the young and watched them pass through the different stages and emerge with wings they are much more easily recognized.

Their Principal Characteristics

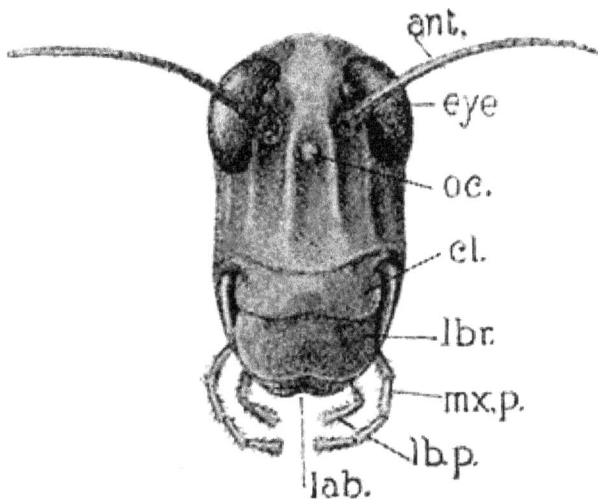

Face of grasshopper enlarged showing parts; ant., antenna; eye, compound eye; oc., ocellus or simple eye; cl., clypeus; lbr., labrum or upper lip; mx. p., maxillary palpus; lb. p., labial palpus; lab., labium or lower lip.

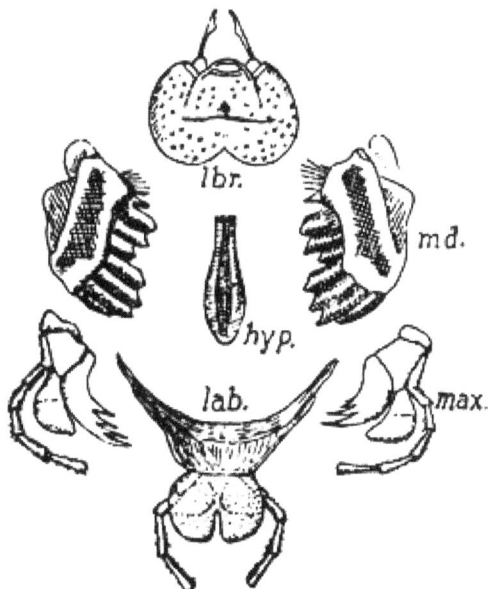

Mouth parts of grasshopper shown in relative position; lbr., labrum; md., mandibles; hyp., hypopharynx; max., maxillae; lab., labium.

Young insects as a rule are soft like caterpillars and maggots, while the old ones usually have a hard body wall, similar to the beetles and wasps. The wings are usually thin and transparent though in some cases they are leathery or hard as in case of beetles or covered with scales as in the butterflies. The three pairs of legs are jointed and used for running, climbing, jumping, swimming, digging or grasping. The feelers or antennae are usually threadlike, clubbed, or resemble a feather and extend forward or sidewise from the head. The large eyes are compound, being made up of many great small units which, when magnified, resemble honey-comb. In some cases two or three small bead-like eyes may be present besides the two large eyes.

The mouth parts of insects may be formed for chewing, as in the grasshopper, or for sucking up liquids, as in the mosquito. The mouth of an insect is built on an entirely different plan from our own. Chewing insects have an upper and lower lip and between these there are two pairs of grinding jaws. These jaws are hinged at the side of the face and when chewing they come together from either side so as to meet in the middle of the mouth. They therefore work sidewise rather than up and down. The mouth parts of the sucking insects are drawn out to form a sucking tube or proboscis as in case of the butterfly or mosquito.

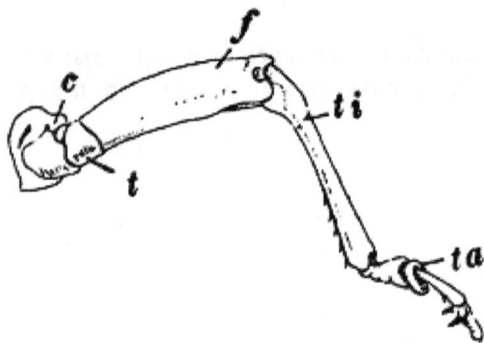

Leg of grasshopper showing segmentation. The basal segment c, is the coxa, the next t, the trochanter, the large segment f, the femur, the long slender one ti, the tibia, and the three jointed tarsus ta, with claws at the tip.

The internal organs of insects are similar to those of other animals. The digestive tube consists of oesophagus, gizzard, or stomach, and intestines. The nervous system is well developed as shown by the extreme sensitiveness of insects to touch. The brain is comparatively small except in the bees and ants. The circulatory system consists simply of a long tube heart, the blood vessels being absent. In this way the internal organs of the insect are simply bathed in the blood. The system of respiration is most complicated. The air is taken in through pores usually along the side of the body and is then carried through fine tracheal tubes to all parts of the body. You cannot drown an insect by putting its head under water, since it does not breathe through its mouth. The muscular system is similar to that of other animals which have the skeleton on the outside.

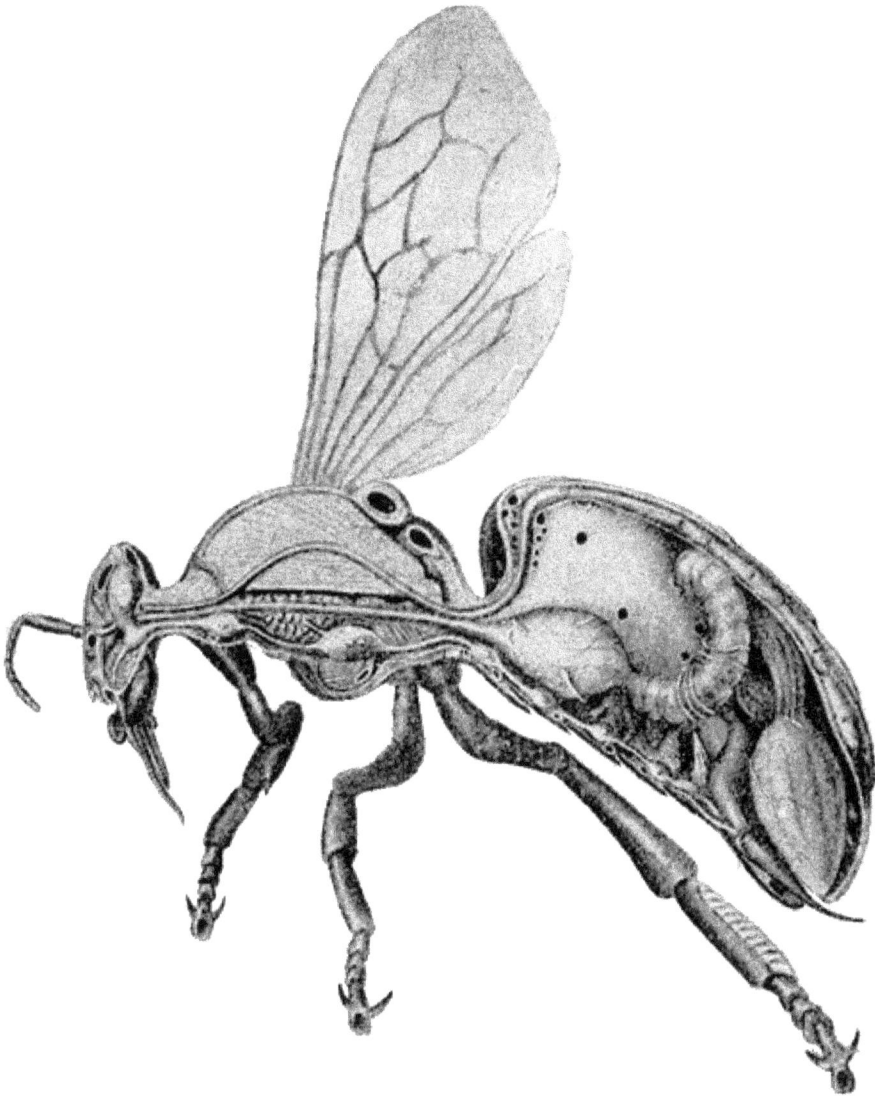

The internal organs of the honey bee. Note the strong wing muscles in the thorax. The tube-like heart begins in the head and extends back through the thorax and follows the curve of the abdomen. Below the heart is the digestive tube consisting of the slender oesophagus which extends back to the expanded honey stomach, in which the bee carries the nectar it collects from flowers, then the curled true stomach, the small intestine and expanded large intestine. Below this is the nervous system consisting of the brain and a chain of connected enlargements or ganglia extending back into the abdomen in the lower part of the body. The respiratory system in part appears just above the honey stomach, and the black circular or oval spots are cross sections of connecting air tubes, which run all through the body. Also note the sting with the poison gland and sack which are pulled out with the sting; also the sucking tube for getting honey from flowers, and the structures on the legs for gathering and carrying pollen; the pollen basket is on the back side of the hind leg.

Their Methods of Developing

In most cases the parent insect deposits small eggs which hatch later into the young insects. In some cases, as with the blow-flies, the maggot may hatch from the egg while yet in the parent's body, when the active larva is born alive. Whether the egg hatches before or after it is deposited, the young insect continues to develop in one of three ways. It may resemble the parent and simply grow as does a kitten, or it may look somewhat like its parent though smaller and without wings, as the young grasshopper, or it may bear no resemblance whatever to the parent, as the caterpillar which feeds and grows and finally spins a cocoon in which it passes to the resting chrysalis stage and later emerges with wings. The development of insects is therefore extremely complicated.

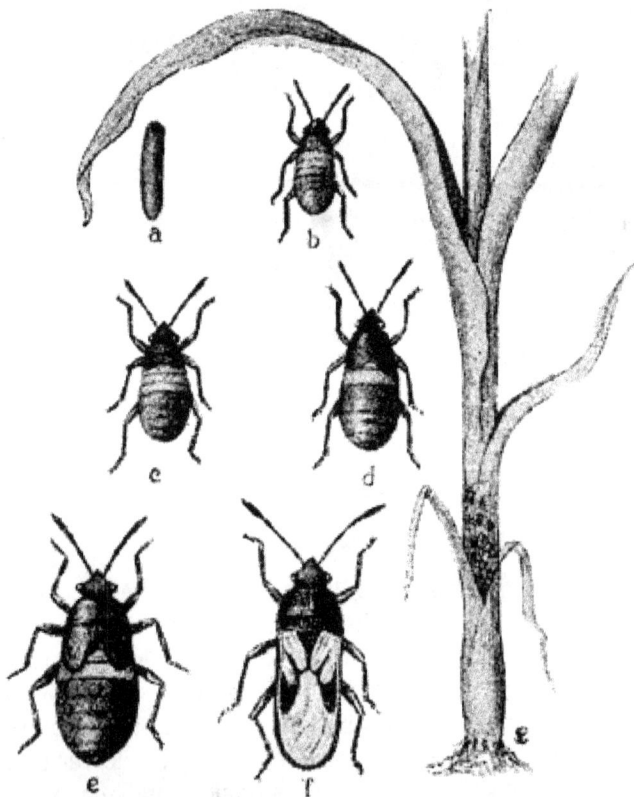

The chinch bug showing development with incomplete metamorphosis; a, egg; b, first nymph; c, second nymph; d, third nymph; e, fourth nymph; f, adult winged bug; g, chinch bugs extracting sap from corn plant. To control this pest burn over all winter harboring places and use chemical or dust barriers following wheat harvest.

The Principal Orders

In order to study a group of animals which includes so many thousand different kinds it is necessary to divide them into a number of sharply defined divisions or orders. All animal life is naturally grouped into such divisions and subdivisions. Among the insects we at once detect seven large, sharply defined divisions or orders, and ten or more smaller ones. Of these we have first, the two-winged true flies; second, the four-winged butterflies and moths; third, the hard-backed beetles; fourth, the stinging four-winged wasps and bees; fifth, the variously formed sucking insects or true bugs, as chinch bugs and bed-bugs; sixth, the rapid-flying four-winged snake doctors or dragon-flies and, seventh, the hopping forms, the grasshoppers. Besides these we have the various smaller orders of water-loving insects, fleas, etc. The seven groups mentioned above include the majority of our common forms and in the studies to follow we will include only representatives from these orders.

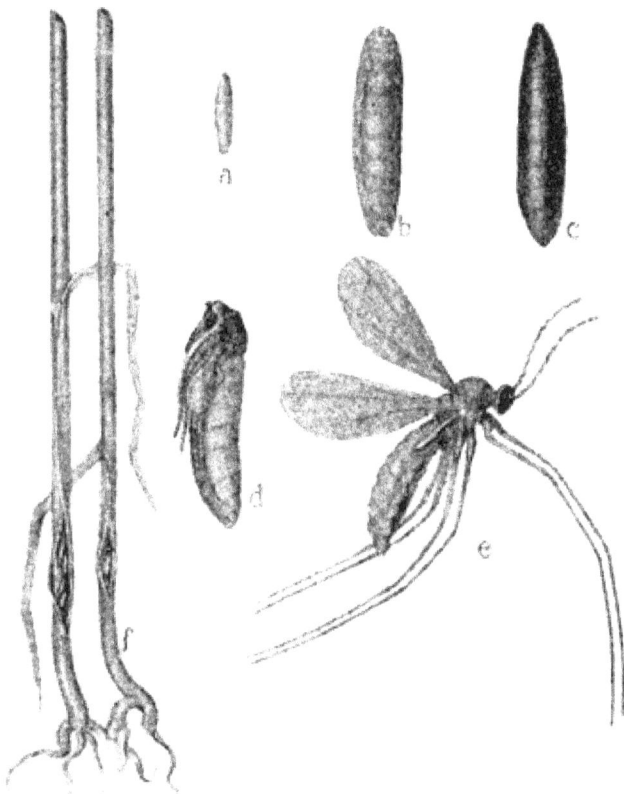

The Hessian fly showing development with complete metamorphosis; a, egg; b, larva or maggot; c, flax-seed stage; d, pupa; e, adult winged fly; f, wheat stubble with flax-seed stages near base taken after harvest. To control this pest, plow under stubble after harvest; keep down all volunteer wheat and sow wheat after fly-free date in the fall.

Their Habits

The habits of insects are as varied as their forms and adaptations. Some live in the water all their life, others spend a part of their life under water, others live the care-free life of the open air, others enjoy feeding upon and living in the foulest of filth, others associate themselves with certain definite crops or animals thereby doing untold injury, while others produce food and other materials which are to be used by man for his comfort. Every imaginable nook and crook, from the depths of lakes to the tops of mountains, from the warm, sunny south to the cold frigid north, from the foul damp swamps to the heart of our desert lands, offers a home for some small insect.

The most striking habits and developments among insects is found in the more highly advanced families of bees and ants where definite insect societies are formed, resembling in many respects human societies and human activities. Among these villages are established, homes built, battles fought, slaves made, herds kept by shepherds, and even fields cultivated. In these groups we have the nearest approach to human intelligence.

Their Role in Agriculture

Some insects may be very destructive to crops, others are beneficial, while the majority of insects are of no importance to man or agriculture. The various forms of pests such as the chinch bug, potato beetles, and others do an enormous amount of damage each year. They destroy hundreds of millions of dollars worth of crops annually in the United States alone. They devour enough to pay for the entire cost of running the school system of our country and nearly enough to meet all the expenses of our government. In view of these facts it is the duty of each and every farmer, young or old, to acquaint himself with these destructive pests and prepare himself for combating them. With a knowledge of the methods of controlling these pests much of this enormous loss can be prevented.

While some insects are extremely injurious, others are very helpful. The products of the honey bee in the United States alone amount to several million dollars a year, to say nothing of its value to the farmer in pollinating fruits. The annual output of silk, all of which is spun by the silkworm, is worth millions of dollars. Many other forms are of value to man by producing material of commercial value such as lac, shellack, dyes, medicines, etc. Of all the beneficial insects those which are of greatest value to man are the parasites and similar forms which help to keep in check many of the severest pests of the farm. Insects are not all bad fellows by any means. One must acquaint himself with those which are good and those which are bad before he can hope to deal with them intelligently.

"And with childlike credulous affection
We behold those tender wings expand,
Emblems of our own great resurrection,
Emblems of the bright and better land."

—LONGFELLOW.

Chapter II

COLLECTING INSECTS

"Does he who searches Nature's secrets scruple
To stick a pin into an insect?"

—A. G. Oehlenschlaeger.

In the life of every normal human there comes a time when he wishes to make a collection of some kind. It may be a collection of coins, postage stamps, post-cards, shells, relics, birds' eggs, pressed flowers or insects. If the child grows up in the country, the result of this craving is usually three or four cigar boxes of insects or an almanac or geography stuffed with the most attractive wild flowers of the field. A collection of this sort may be small and poorly kept and yet it is worth while. In later life one will search in his mother's closet or attic for the old cigar boxes which contain the remains of youthful efforts, usually a mass of gaudy wings, fragments of insect legs and bodies and a few rusty pins. This desire to make a collection is natural and should be encouraged in the child. It tends to make him observe closely and creates an interest in things about him, and if properly directed it will add a store of information which can be gotten in no other way.

Directions for Collecting

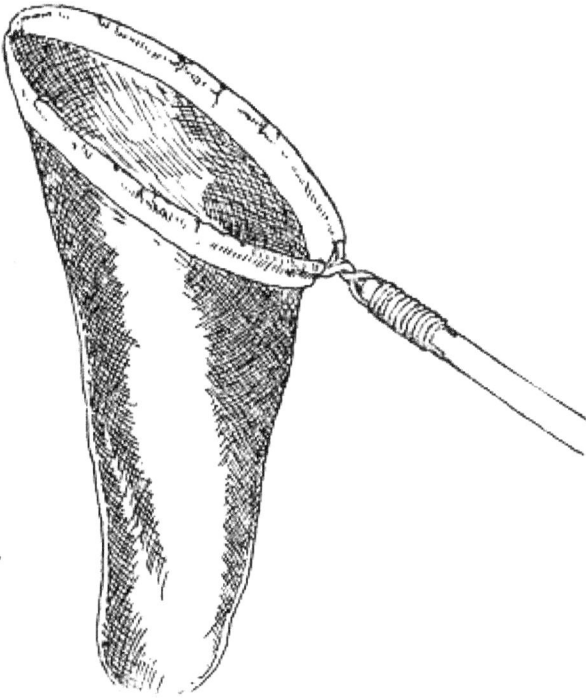

A convenient home-made net for catching insects; note the broom-stick handle, heavy twisted wire and mosquito net bag.

A cyanide jar for killing insects; note the lumps of the deadly poison potassium cyanide in the bottom covered and sealed by a layer of plaster of Paris.

Many boys and girls of the rural schools will have little time or inclination to provide themselves with apparatus for collecting insects. An old straw hat or a limb will serve their purpose. From their point of view what difference does it make if they tear off most of the legs and break the wings? They succeed in securing the "bug" and when pinned in the box it will mean just about as much to them as the most perfect specimen ever prepared.

This method of catching insects will prove effective where nothing better is available, but any child can easily make a small insect net by attaching a loop of fairly stiff wire to a broom handle or other stick and sewing a bag of mosquito netting or other thin cloth to the wire. By means of such a net one can catch insects more easily and at the same time there is less danger of tearing such insects as butterflies. Care must be taken in handling the stinging insects.

The country boy and girl will have little trouble getting hold of insects, but they are often puzzled when it comes to killing them. It seems cruel to pin up an insect alive and have it squirm for a day or two and some means of killing them should be devised. Most of the soft insects, such as flies, butterflies, etc., can be killed by pressing their body, in the region of the wings, between one's thumb and forefinger. Such forms as beetles and wasps can be quickly killed by dropping them into coal oil or a strong soap suds. Any method which can be devised for quickly killing the insect, and which will not seriously mutilate it, can be used.

A convenient killing bottle can be made by sealing a few small lumps of the deadly poison, potassium or sodium cyanide, in the bottom of a strong, wide-mouthed bottle, with plaster of Paris; or a few drops of chloroform or ether on a wad of cotton in a similar bottle, will also serve as a convenient killing jar.

Pinning and Preserving a Collection

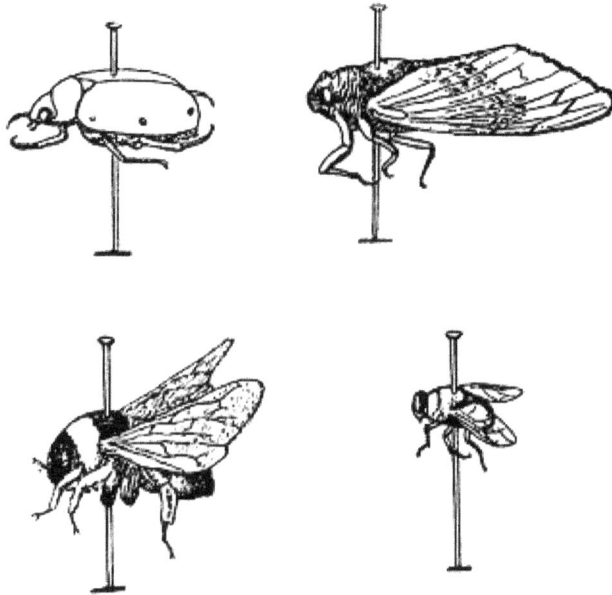

Method of pinning different kinds of insects.

After the insects, have been caught and killed, they should then be prepared for the permanent collection. Most insects such as wasps, beetles, flies and grasshoppers should simply have a pin thrust through their bodies until they are two-thirds the way up on the pin and then put them away in a box. Such forms as butterflies and moths make a much better collection if the wings are spread so as to bring out their gaudy markings. In order to spread butterflies' wings, one needs a spreading board, which can be made in ten minutes by taking a pine board two feet long, and six inches wide and on this nail two strips an inch thick, so that there is a crack between them. The crack should be half an inch wide at one end and a quarter of an inch wide at the other end, and in the bottom of it press strips of cornstalk pith so as to have something soft in which to stick the pins. After a pin has been stuck through the body of a dead butterfly between the wings, it is then pinned in the crack so that the back of the butterfly is on a level with the strips. Then the wings are drawn forward until they stand straight out from the body when they are pinned down by means of strips of paper and left to dry a few days until they become perfectly rigid. In this way a most beautiful collection can be made very easily, but where time and materials are not available, simply pin them up like other insects, leaving the wings to hang as they will. After the specimens are pinned they should be put away in cigar boxes in the bottom of which is pinned or pasted a layer of cork or corrugated paper similar to that which comes between glass fruit cans. These make ideal cases for keeping small collections as the odor of tobacco helps keep pests from getting in to destroy the collection.

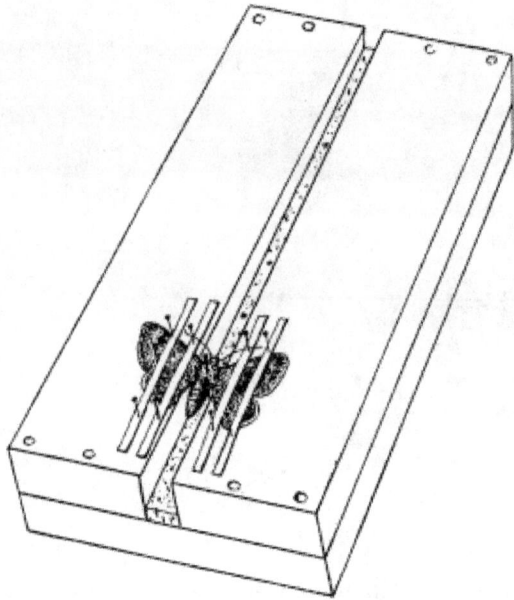

Home-made spreading board for spreading butterflies and moths.

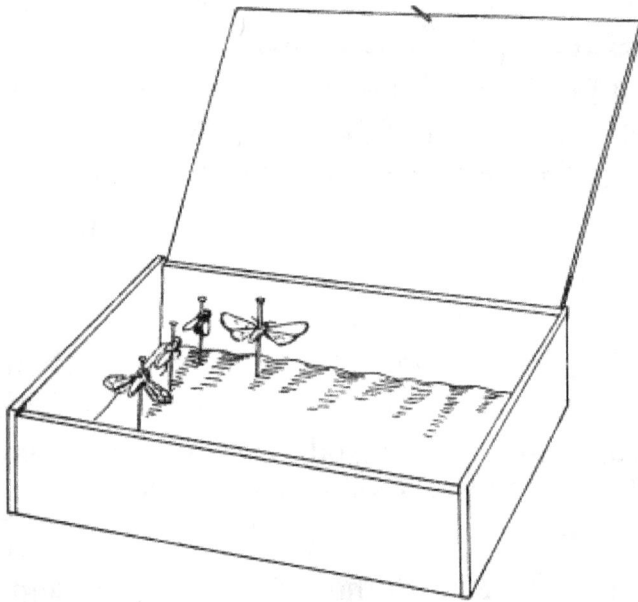

Cigar box with strip of corrugated paper in bottom used as case for keeping pinned insects.

Rearing and Observing Them While Alive

While studying an insect it is advisable wherever possible to first study it where it is found in the field and later bring it home and keep it alive in a jar where it can be fed and observed and its various habits studied. Cages for breeding insects consist simply of a few glass fruit cans and jelly glasses with tin or cloth covers. A child can borrow one or two of these from his mother's fruit cellar. A layer of moist sand or soil should be put in the bottom of the jar to provide a retreat for those forms which go into the ground before changing to adults. Before an insect is placed in one of these breeding cages its food plant should be determined by observations in the field, and every day or two a fresh supply should be gathered. Most of the forms discussed in the following chapters can be kept in jars and reared to the adult stage. Rearing insects is both interesting and instructive. Every child should be given an opportunity to rear a few forms either during the school year or during the summer vacation.

"I happened one night in my travels
    To stray into Butterfly Vale,
Where my wondering eyes beheld butterflies
    WITH WINGS THAT WERE WIDE AS A SAIL.
They lived in such houses of grandeur,
    Their days were successions of joys,
And the very last fad these butterflies had
    WAS MAKING COLLECTIONS OF BOYS.

"There were boys of all sizes and ages
    PINNED UP ON THEIR WALLS. *When I said*
'Twas a terrible sight to see boys in that plight,
    I was answered: 'OH, WELL THEY ARE DEAD.
WE CATCH THEM ALIVE, BUT WE KILL THEM,
    WITH ETHER—A VERY NICE WAY:
Just look at this fellow—his hair is so yellow,
    And his eyes such a beautiful gray.

"'Then there is a droll little darky,
    As black as the clay at our feet;
He sets off that blond that is pinned just beyond
    In a way most artistic and neat.
And now let me show you the latest,—
    A specimen really select,
A boy with a head that is carroty-red

And a face that is funnily specked.

"'We cannot decide where to place him;
    Those spots bar him out of each class;
We think him a treasure to study at leisure
    And analyze under a glass.'
I seemed to grow cold as I listened
    To the words that these butterflies spoke;
With fear overcome, I was speechless and dumb,
    And then with a start,—I awoke!"

—Ella Wheeler Wilcox.

CHAPTER III

THE GRASSHOPPER

THE grasshopper or locust is one of the most ancient plagues of cultivated crops. From the earliest time they have destroyed crops. During Moses' sojourn in Egypt they were so destructive as to cause severe famine and various other references to their destructive work are to be found in the early writings. Since those early days, just think of the crops that have disappeared between the greedy jaws of grasshoppers!

In our own country it has not been many years since the sun was darkened for days by clouds of grasshoppers as they settled down from the Rocky Mountains upon the growing crops in the neighboring states. One day a field might have a promising crop and by the next day it might be left as bare as a dry stubble field in August. Those days of great destruction in America have largely passed but each year the active jaws of "hoppers" devour a handsome fortune.

Common differential locust or grasshopper; a, egg nests underground; b, young nymph; c, d, older nymphs; e, adult grasshopper; f, nymph feeding on grass. This shows development with incomplete metamorphosis.

In the same order with the grasshoppers come the crickets, katydids, rear-horses, devil's darning-needles or walking-sticks, and cockroaches. The grasshoppers are most troublesome, however. They deposit eggs in the ground and in other protected places. In the spring these hatch into young "hoppers" scarcely larger than a pin head at first. Throughout the early summer these small fellows feed and increase in size. They burst their old skins and crawl out of them a number of times as they grow larger. Toward fall they become full grown with four strong wings and very powerful hind legs for jumping. In this condition most of the common grasshoppers will be found in the fall when the rural schools open.

FIELD STUDIES

The small so-called red-legged grasshopper is always most abundant in the fall and for this reason we have selected it for our studies. It is about an inch long, olive-brown in color with the ends of the hind legs bright red. It is found everywhere in pastures, meadows and along country roads. Approach one of them in the field and see what happens. How does it get away? When disturbed, how far does it go? Does it hide in the grass when you try to catch it? Observe one that has not been disturbed. Where do you find it; on the ground or on plants? How does it move about when not scared? Watch carefully and see what plants it feeds on. How does it go about it? What do you find feeding on grasshoppers? How does a turkey catch them? Have you ever seen a dull colored fly, which inhabits dry paths and which flies with a humming sound like a bee, feeding on grasshoppers? These are called "robber-flies" or "spider-hawks" and they destroy thousands of grasshoppers.

BREEDING CAGE OBSERVATIONS

After you have learned all you can about the habits of the grasshopper in the field, catch a few of them and take them home and put them in a glass fruit jar. Collect green leaves for them and watch them feed. Watch their method of feeding closely and see how it differs from that of a horse or a cow. How do they move about in the jar? Which legs are used in walking? What do they do with the jumping legs while walking? Do they use their wings at all while in the jar? Watch them wash their face and feet after feeding. Give them leaves of different plants, especially of field and garden crops and determine which they like best. Can you find any plant which they will not eat? Find out how fast they feed and considering the life of any one individual to be 200 days, calculate the number of grass blades each individual may eat. Are the feelers used while in the jar, and if so for what purpose?

STUDY OF SPECIMEN

Take a grasshopper from the jar and examine it carefully. Count the number of legs, wings and joints in the body. How many joints in the legs? Examine the tip of the foot for a soft pad and on either side of it a strong hook. What are these used for? What are the sharp spines on the side of the hind-legs for? Examine the side of the body and see if you can find the small breathing pores. How do the legs join the body? Where are the wings attached? How broad are the wings as compared with the body? How are they folded? Are the two pairs of wings alike? Which is used most in flying? Is the head firmly attached to the body? Examine the large eyes; where are they found? Will grasshoppers bite you while handling them? What is the brown juice which escapes from the mouth when disturbed? How long are the feelers as compared with the body? Can you tell the males from the females? What is the distinction? Do they ever make music? Examine for all the foregoing points and write a brief report covering these. Make a careful drawing of a grasshopper from one side; also make an enlarged drawing of the face of a grasshopper and name the parts.

CHAPTER IV

THE HOUSE FLY OR TYPHOID FLY

IN the house fly we find one of man's most deadly foes. War can not compare with the campaigns of disease and death waged by this most filthy of all insects. In our recent strife with Spain we lost a few lives in battle, but we lost many more in hospitals due to contagious diseases, in the transmission of which this pest played a most important part.

The fly is dangerous on account of its filthy habits. It breeds in filth, feeds on filth in open closets, slop-barrels, on the streets and in back alleys and then comes into the house and wipes this germ-laden filth on our food or on the hands or even in the mouths of helpless babies. Who has not seen flies feeding on running sores on animals, or on "spit" on sidewalks? These same flies the next minute may be feeding on fruits or other food materials. We rebel when pests destroy our crops or attack our stock, but here we have a pest which endangers our very lives, and the lives of those dear to us.

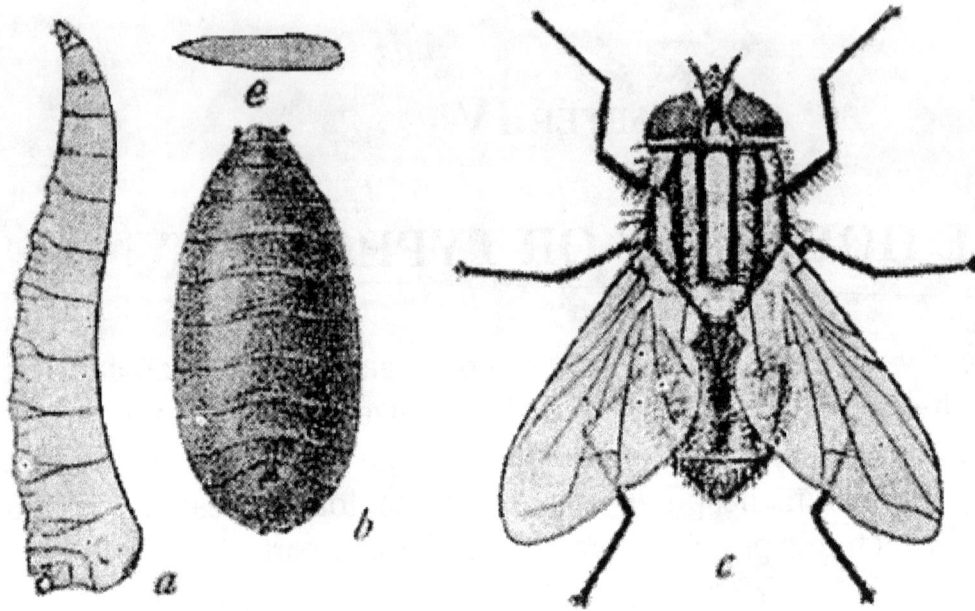

House fly; a, larva or maggot; b, pupa; c, adult; e, egg. All enlarged. (Modified from Howard Bur. of Entomology. U. S. Dept. Agri.)

If the fly confined itself to filth we could overlook it as it would help to hasten the removal of filth. On the other hand, if it avoided filth and remained in our home we could not overlook it, but we could feel safe that it was not apt to do us a great deal of harm. But, like the English sparrow, one minute it is here and the next somewhere else; from filth to foods and then back again to filth. In this way it carries disease germs upon its feet and other parts of its body and by coming in contact with food material some of these germs are sure to be left on it and cause trouble later. The fly's method of carrying disease is different from that of the mosquito where the germ is carried inside its body.

Favorite breeding places of house fly. Such places should be kept as clean and neat as the front yard.

The presence of flies in the home is usually a sign of untidiness; but it means more, it means that disease and often death is hovering over the home. We are too apt to consider the fly simply as a nuisance when we should take it more seriously. The child should be led to realize that the fly should not be tolerated in the home, that it is dangerous and that it can and must be destroyed.

An open closet to which the house fly has free access. Such a closet is the most dangerous accessory of any home.

The house fly may pass the winter either as the adult fly in cracks and crannies about the home, or in out-buildings or it may remain as a hard, brown, oval pupa in stables and manure piles when, with the first warm days of spring, it escape from this case as the fly ready to lay eggs for the first colony. The fly breeds largely in horse manure either in stables, manure piles or in street gutters where manure is allowed to collect. Each female lays a large number of eggs and since it requires less than two weeks for the pest to mature, we are soon overrun with flies in the summer where steps are not taken to control them. The maggots are often so abundant in stables that they can be scooped out with a shovel. This ceaseless breeding continues from spring until the first frost in the fall.

In the control of the fly and prevention of trouble from it there are three important steps to take. First of all, go to the source of the trouble and do away with or screen all breeding places. Then, by keeping in mind the fact that the fly is comparatively harmless as long as it is kept from filth laden with germs, do away with all open closets, uncovered slop-barrels and other filth. As a further precaution keep it from the home by the use of screens and when necessary "swatters." Do not make the mistake of trying to control the pest with the "swatters" alone. In the country too often manure is permitted to accumulate about the barn during the summer with a view of using it on wheat ground in the fall and this furnishes ideal conditions for the fly to breed. Another source of constant danger especially in the rural districts is the presence of open closets or worse still the presence of no closet at all. This is without doubt the most dangerous accessory of the farm. More screens should be used in the home and greater care in keeping them closed.

Study of the Fly and Its Work

Observe first of all the feeding habits of the fly. What foods in the home is it most fond of? Make a list of all the food materials it is found to feed on. Where and on what is it found feeding out doors? Do you find it feeding on filth and if so, on what? Do you find it about the barn? Where is it usually found in the barn? How can the fly carry filth to food materials?

In studying the breeding of the fly determine where it lays its eggs and where the maggots are found. Examine fresh manure in the stable and see if you can find small white maggots about half an inch long and as large around as the lead in a pencil. If you do, place some of them with some fresh manure in a glass jar and see what becomes of them. In a few days the maggots will disappear and in their places small oval, brown bean-like objects will appear. A few days later these will crack open at one end and the fly will crawl out. Keep records of the length of time it requires for the pest to pass from one stage to the other. If maggots cannot be gotten put some fresh manure in the jar and catch a number of live house flies and put them in with the manure and watch for results. Collect a jar of fresh manure with maggots and sift over it a little powdered borax and see what happens to the maggots. Where horse manure can not be properly disposed of, cheap borax is used to throw over piles of manure to destroy the maggots and prevent the flies from breeding in it. Write a brief description of the different stages and make careful drawings of these. Do not mistake the house fly for other flies often found on food in the home.

Collect a few flies and put them in a bottle and drop in with them just a few crumbs of sugar and watch them feed. They cannot chew but a little saliva from the mouth dissolves a little of the sugar which is then lapped up as syrup. Notice what a peculiar sucker they have for drawing up liquids. How can they crawl along in the bottle with their backs toward the floor? Examine the tip of their feet for a small glue pad which sticks to the glass. These glue pads and the sucker are well fitted for carrying filth. Examine the fly carefully and write a brief description of it. What color is it? How many legs? How many wings? Are these transparent? Behind the wings there is a pair of small stubs which is all that is left of the hind pair of wings. Are the eyes large? Can you find a pair of small feelers? Why can you not pick up a fly like you would a grasshopper? Is their eye sight good? Why are they always most abundant on a kitchen screen door? Can they smell?

What are the fly's worst enemies? Will the toad eat them? Do chickens eat them? Have you ever seen chickens scratching in manure and feeding on the fly maggots? Put a few drops of formaldehyde, which you can get from a druggist, in a few spoonfuls of sweet milk or sugar syrup and let the flies eat it and see what happens to them. This is one of our best poison baits for flies which get in the home or collect about the dairy. Formaldehyde is a poison and when used in bait it must be kept out of reach of children. Just about frost, in the fall, watch for the appearance of inactive flies on walls, windows and other parts of the house. These have been attacked by a parasitic disease. These are often found sticking to walls and other objects about the room in the winter, and are commonly thought to be passing the winter.

"The insect we now call the 'house fly' should in the future be termed the 'typhoid fly,' in order to call direct attention to the danger of allowing it to continue to breed unchecked."

—L. O. HOWARD.

CHAPTER V

THE MOSQUITO

HERE we have another small insect which, like the house fly, is extremely dangerous, due to its ability to carry the germs of disease. There are hundreds of species of mosquitoes, some small, some large. The majority of these are unable to carry disease so far as we know at present, but they should be avoided as dangerous. The Missouri forms which carry disease are the so-called malarial fever mosquitoes, and they are entirely responsible for the transmission of this sapping and often fatal disease. In the warm countries these are more abundant and the fever is more fatal. In the south there is still another disease-carrying mosquito, the yellow fever mosquito. This form is most dangerous of all.

The mosquito first bites a patient suffering with malaria and in this way it takes in germs along with the blood which it sucks from the patient. After these germs pass through stages of development in the body of the mosquito they are ready to be injected back into a healthy person where, in due time, they cause the disease. The germs feed inside the red blood corpuscles and at regular intervals they destroy a large number of these causing a chill which is followed by fever and a new supply of corpuscles is produced. This alternation of chill and fever may continue all summer, if medicine is not taken to destroy the germs. Quinine will kill the germs if it is taken so that plenty of it is in the blood when the germs come out of the torn down corpuscles during a chill.

In order to prevent malarial fever, get rid of the mosquitoes by draining and oiling the breeding places, escape their bites by screening houses, smudging and destroying the adults, and keep the mosquitoes from patients who have the fever. This is almost as important as the destruction of the mosquitoes. The malarial fever mosquitoes are as harmless as our common forms so long as they do not become infected with germs by sucking blood from a fever patient.

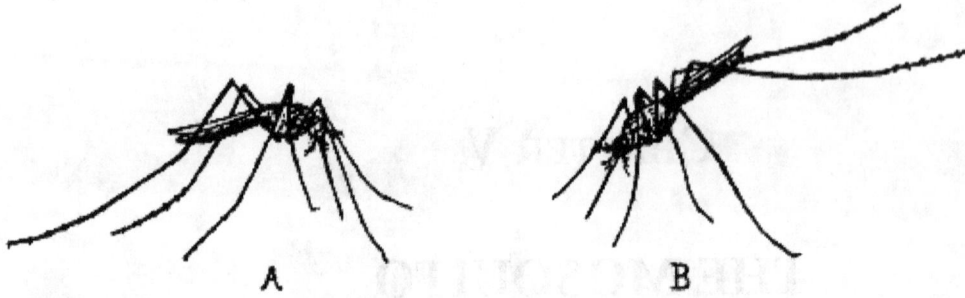

Mosquitoes in position for biting; a, common Culex mosquito; b, malarial fever mosquito. Note that the one stands parallel, while the other stands at an angle to the surface on which it rests.

In view of the fact that most of our common mosquitoes are classed as non-dangerous, it is of interest to know just how to distinguish the harmless ones from the dangerous. The adults of the two forms can be easily distinguished when they are seen at rest. The common forms always rest with the body parallel to the surface on which they rest, while the malarial form always elevates the end of the body so that the head is pointed toward the surface on which it rests. In like manner the wigglers can be distinguished from each other. Our common wigglers always hang head downward in the water while those of the malarial mosquitoes rest near the surface of the water with their bodies parallel to it. The majority of the wigglers found in rain barrels are of our common forms.

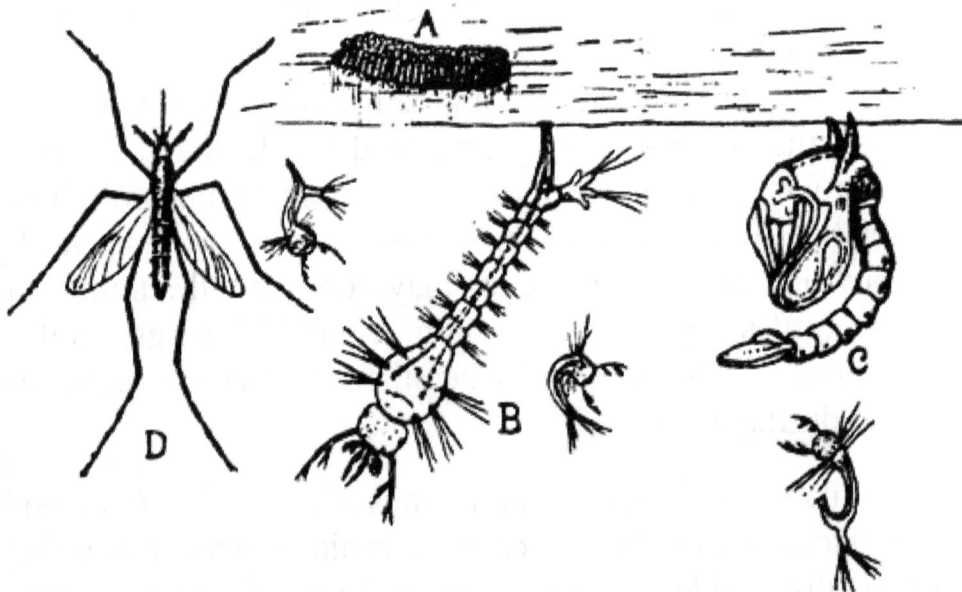

Common Culex mosquito showing stages of development; a, raft of eggs; b, larvæ or wigglers of different sizes; c, pupa; d, mosquito. The large wiggler and the pupa are taking air from the surface of the water through their breathing tubes.

The life of the mosquito is quite interesting and is an excellent example of an insect which lives in the water part of its life and in the air the rest. The mature female mosquito, which does all the biting, searches for water in rain barrels, cans, ditches, ponds, and stagnant swamps where she lays her eggs either in raft-shaped packets or singly. When the wigglers hatch they swim about in the water and feed upon decaying material and microscopic water plants. When the wiggler is full grown it changes to an active pupa which has a large head and a slender tail and is more or less coiled. A little later the winged mosquito escapes. In the rural districts most of the mosquitoes breed in stagnant ponds, swamps and rain barrels and from these they fly to the home where they cause trouble. Such places should be drained or protected with oil or other means to prevent the mosquito from using them for breeding purposes. Ponds can be freed of the wigglers by introducing fish or by using a small amount of coal oil on the surface. The wigglers have a breathing tube which is thrust out above the water when fresh air is needed and if there is a thin film of oil on the water this is prevented. Rain barrels can be freed of the pest in this way also, or perhaps better by covering them with a cloth. The mosquitoes are most troublesome about the home at night. When one sits out doors he should keep a smudge going to drive them away while screens will keep them out of the house at night.

Observations and Study

Collect all the different kinds of mosquitoes you can find and note difference in size and markings. Do you find the malarial fever mosquito in your region? Is malarial fever common during the summer and fall? Are there any old stagnant ponds or swamps near your home? If so, examine these for wigglers. Examine rain barrels for small raft-shaped packets of eggs. These resemble small flakes of soot and are difficult to pick up between your fingers. Take a stick and lift them from the water and examine them. One packet may contain a hundred or more eggs. Put a few of these packets in a tumbler of rain water and watch for the wigglers. At first they will be very small but they grow fast. Watch them come to the surface to breathe. The tip of the tail is projected above the water and air is taken in at two small breathing pores or spiracles. Examine rain barrels for the larger wigglers. What do they live on in the rain barrel? What do they do when you jar the barrel? Do you find any of the rounded pupae in the barrel? They are active the same as the wigglers. If you find pupae, put some in a tumbler of water, cover it with cloth or a lid and watch for the mosquitoes to appear. After collecting several mosquitoes examine them for number of wings, legs and markings and see if all have the slender sucking tube. The males have large feathery feelers, but no sucking tube.

Write a brief description of the wiggler and the mosquito, their breeding places and means of destroying them. Make drawings of the different stages, wiggler, pupa and mosquito.

CHAPTER VI

THE CABBAGE MILLER

*"And here and yonder a flaky butterfly
Was doubting in the air."*

—McDONALD.

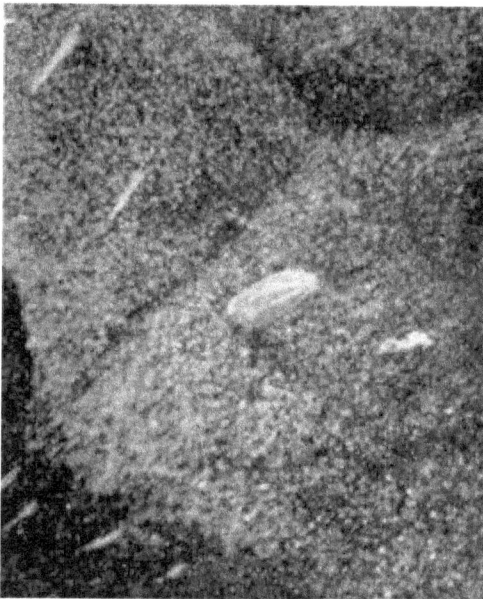

Egg of cabbage miller much enlarged.

W ITH the first approach of spring comes swarms of large green flies which bask in the March sun on the south sides of buildings. They are not with us long, however, until we notice flashes of white quickly moving about from one early weed to another. These are the advance guards of the cabbage millers or butterflies. All through the cold winter they remained in the chrysalis stage stuck to the sides of houses, fence posts and in other protected places, awaiting the first breath of spring. The first adults to emerge find no cabbage on which to lay their eggs so they are compelled to use other plants such as pepper grass.

The eggs are very small and are usually placed on the lower edge of the leaf. These hatch and the small green worms appear. Throughout the summer there are a number of broods produced and an enormous amount of damage is done. Just before frost the last caterpillars search for protected places where they pass to the pupal or resting stage for the winter. No cocoon is spun by this caterpillar.

Where measures are not taken to control the cabbage worms they destroy much of the cabbage crop each season. The white butterflies can be seen any day during the summer visiting cabbage, mustard, radishes and other similar plants. By destroying all of the worms and millers in the early spring one has less trouble later. This can be done by hand picking, or where the patch is large by spraying with a poison solution to which soap is added to keep the solution from rolling off in large drops. Poison can be used until the heads are well formed, but if the first worms in the spring are destroyed, later spraying is unnecessary though an occasional handpicking will help.

OBSERVATIONS AND STUDY

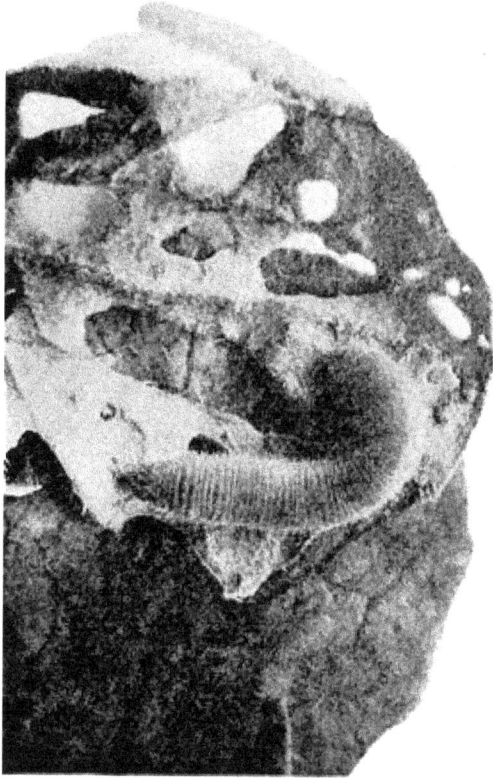
Cabbage worm feeding, slightly enlarged.

Pupa or chrysalis of cabbage miller.

Go into the garden and examine the cabbage for small green worms which vary from one fourth to a little over an inch in length. What is the nature of their work on the leaf? Where do they feed most, on the outer or inner leaves? Do they eat the entire leaf? How does the work of the young worms differ from that of the larger ones? Do they spin silk? Are they on the top or under side of the leaf? Examine under the dead and dried leaves at the ground and see if you can find small, hard, gray objects which have sharp angles and which are tied to the leaf with a cord of silk. What are these objects? Watch the miller as she visits the cabbage and see if you can find the small eggs which she lays on the under side of the leaves. When she visits a cabbage plant she bends her body up under the outer leaves and stops but a moment, fluttering all the while as she sticks the small egg to the leaf. It is about the size of a small crumb of bread. What does the miller feed on? Does she visit flowers? If so, what flowers?

BREEDING WORK

Collect a few of the worms and put them in a glass jar with a piece of cabbage leaf. Examine them carefully and watch them crawl. How many legs do they have? Where are they placed on the body? How can they use so many legs while crawling? How many joints are there to the body? Note the short fine hair all over the body which gives it the appearance of green velvet. What color is the head? How does the caterpillar feed? Write a brief description of the worm. Do not mistake it for the cabbage span-worm which is also green, but which walks by humping up its back.

Cabbage miller on red clover blossom.

Keep the cabbage worms in the jar for a few days and watch them disappear. After they have disappeared, what is left in the jar? These are the chrysalids or pupae of the insect and later from them will come the millers. Take one of the pupae in your hand and see if it can move. If it is in the summer the miller will appear in a week, but if it is in the late fall it will simply pass the winter in the pupa stage. Watch the miller escape from the pupal case and describe it. Examine the miller carefully and describe briefly the number of legs, wings, segments of body, sucking tube and color markings. Make careful drawings of the caterpillar, chrysalis and butterfly. What gives the color to the wings? Rub the wings between your fingers and see if the color comes off. The wings are covered with very small scales of different colors which combine to give the beautiful markings. The wings of all butterflies and moths are covered with scales and hairs in this way. In this insect we find both chewing and sucking mouth parts. The caterpillar chews while the parent butterfly has a long tube for sucking up nectar from flowers and water from puddles in the road.

"Far out at sea—the sun was high,
 While veered the wind and flapped the sail;
We saw a snow-white butterfly
 Dancing before the fitful gale
  Far out at sea.

"The little wanderer, who had lost
 His way, of danger nothing knew;
Settled a while upon the mast;
 Then fluttered o'er the waters blue
  Far out at sea.

"Above, there gleamed the boundless sky;
 Beneath, the boundless ocean sheen;
Between them danced the butterfly,
 The spirit-life of this vast scene,
  Far out at sea.

"The tiny soul that soared away,
 Seeking the clouds on fragile wings,
Lured by the brighter, purer ray
 Which hope's ecstatic morning brings—
  Far out at sea.

"Away he sped, with shimmering glee,
 Scarce seen, now lost, yet onward borne!
Night comes with wind and rain, and he
 No more will dance before the morn,
  Far out at sea.

"He dies, unlike his mates, I ween
 Perhaps not sooner or worse crossed;

And he hath felt and known and seen
A larger life and hope, though lost
Far out at sea."

—R. H. HORNE.

CHAPTER VII

THE APPLE WORM

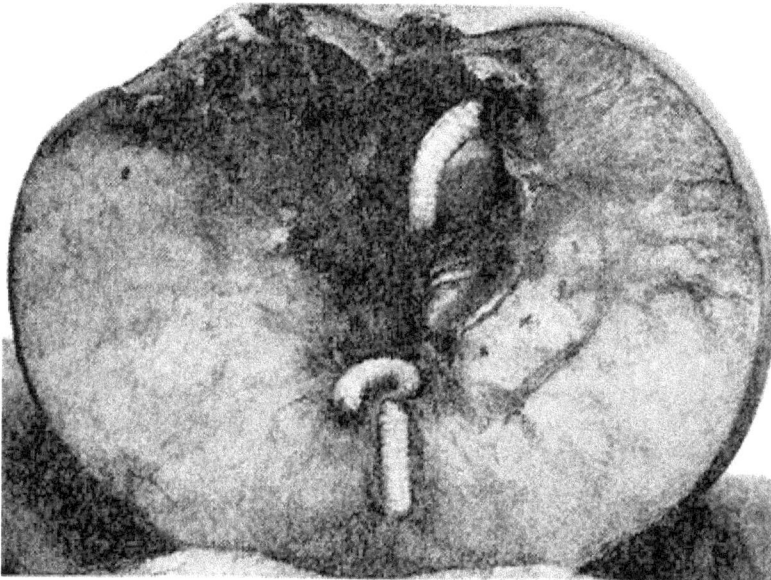

Apple worms in core of apple.
Usually only one worm appears in an apple. Note the decaying of the apple.

THIS is perhaps the most destructive insect pest attacking the apple. Every year, that we have a good apple crop, there are thousands of bushels of wormy apples which are practically worthless. This means an actual loss of thousands of dollars a year to the apple growers of this country. For this reason alone each child should come to know the life history, habits and injury of this pest. It is most destructive to the apple though the pear comes in for its share.

The codling moth slightly enlarged. (From Slingerland).

Every country child and many of those of the cities, are familiar with this worm for they often bite into it while eating apples. The small worms crawl down in the blossom end of the young developing apple and from there bore into the pulp and eventually reach the core of the fruit. They stay in the apple about six weeks when they eat a hole out to the surface and crawl down to the trunk where loose bark offers a hiding place. Here they spin their cocoons and change to a small, brown, plump pupa and after a few days the winged moth emerges. The moth is very small and is not often found by one not acquainted with it. They come out during late June and early July when they lay eggs for a second colony of worms which again enter the fruit and destroy more of it. These worms of the second brood are usually mature and leave the fruit about the time apples are picked in the fall in central Missouri. They escape and soon spin cocoons in which they pass the winter. Early in the spring these change to pupae and later the moths come out. They appear about the time apples bloom in the spring and lay the eggs for the first worms which enter in great numbers at the blossom end.

Apple blossoms at about the right stage for receiving the first and most important arsenical spray for the control of the apple worm.

This in short, is the life story of the pest through the year. Little can be done to destroy the pest after it gets into the fruit, therefore remedies must be applied to destroy the worm before it gets into the fruit. All orchards should be sprayed with a poison in the spring before the worms appear. Since most of them enter by way of the blossom end, it is necessary that the poison be put into the blossom end. To do this spray at once after the blossoms fall, repeat after two weeks and spray again in July to kill the second brood of worms. The protection of woodpeckers and sapsuckers will also help as they feed on the worms under the bark.

OBSERVATIONS AND BREEDING WORK

Go into the orchard and examine for apples with masses of sawdust-like material projecting from the sides or blossom end. By removing this brown deposit which is the excrement of the worm, you will find a hole leading into the apple. Cut open one of these and determine the course of the tunnel. Where do you find the worm? Do all such apples contain worms? Where have they gone? How does the feeding of the worms injure the fruit? Do any of the wormy apples show rot? Are any of the windfalls in the orchard wormy and if so what proportion?

Remove a worm from one of the apples and examine it. How many legs has it? What color is it and does it have hair upon its body? Can it crawl fast? Does it spin silk? Put a number of the large worms in a jar and examine from day to day and keep records of what happens. Collect a number in the fall and keep them in a box outdoors during the winter. In the spring watch them change to the pupa in the cocoon and a little later the mature insect or codling moth, as it is commonly called, will emerge. Describe the moth and pin a number of them for your collection. What time in the spring do the caterpillars change to the pupa and when do the moths emerge? If you keep the moths in a bottle they will lay their small circular flat eggs where they can be seen by looking closely. During the winter examine under the bark of apple trees and in cracks and crevices about apple pens for the small silk cocoons containing the worms. Examine in the same places in the spring about apple blooming time and then in place of the small pink worms you will find the small brown pupae. Keep these a few days and the moths will appear.

What proportion of apples in your region are wormy? What are they used for? Are the trees sprayed just after the blossoms fall to control the pest? Where spraying is carefully done, are there as many wormy apples? Why not spray all the orchards properly and have no worms?

Draw and describe the different stages of the apple worm or codling moth and its injury to fruit.

"O, yet we trust that somehow good
    Will be the final goal of ill,
To pangs of nature, sins of will,
    Defects of doubt and taints of blood;

"That nothing walks with aimless feet;
    That not one life shall be destroyed,
Or cast as rubbish to the void,
    When God hath made the pile complete;

"That not a worm is cloven in vain,
    That not a moth with vain desire,
Is shrivelled in a fruitless fire,
    Or but subserves another's gain."

—TENNYSON.

Chapter VIII

THE TOMATO OR TOBACCO WORM

THIS insect is often very destructive to tomatoes and tobacco. Most country boys and girls know it and fear its ugly looking horn. When full grown it is four inches long, usually dark green with a number of slanting white lines along either side. It is so near the color of the plants that it is difficult to see it.

Egg of Tomato worm moth enlarged.

During the summer months the worms are common, being most abundant in August. In the fall the mature worms go into the ground and change from the worm to a large, oval, brown pupa with a jug-handle-like appendage on the under side. These are often turned up when the garden is plowed in the spring. After tomato plants are well started the large greyish humming-bird-like moths comes from the ground and begin laying eggs. The moth expands from four to six inches and is often seen at dusk visiting the blossoms of "jimson weed" and other large tube flowers. They are also found around lights at night.

Young tomato worm.

Where they are troublesome the plants should either be sprayed with a poison when the injury is first noticed or else the worms should be picked off and destroyed. There is a small parasitic wasp which is very helpful in destroying this caterpillar. They live inside the worm and when mature bore out through the skin on the sides and back where they spin small white egg-like cocoons from which later the small wasps emerge. Often a hundred or more may come out of one worm.

STUDY AND OBSERVATION

Observe the worms where they are at work on tomatoes. Disturb them and hear them grind their jaws together. Do they eat the foliage rapidly? Dust a little Paris green on the foliage where a worm is eating and see what happens in half an hour. Collect a number of the worms in a glass fruit can and give them tomato leaves to eat and watch them grow. How many segments are there to the body? How many of the segments have small black spots on either side? These are holes through which the worm breathes. Is the horn at the end of the body stiff enough to stick into your hand? This is thought to be a sting but it is only an ornament and is entirely harmless. When full grown they will burrow into the sand in the jar and change to the pupa.

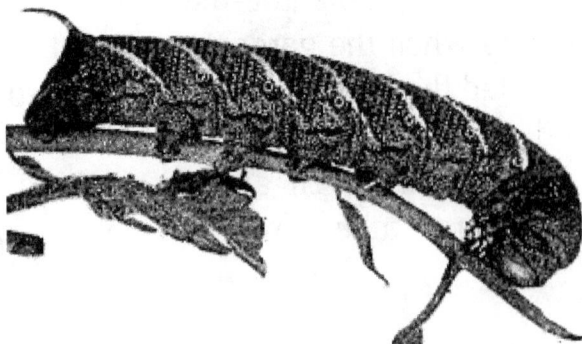

Full-fed tomato worm slightly reduced.

Chrysalis or pupa of tomato worm. Note the jug-handle-like sheaths enclosing the proboscis.

Examine the brown pupa carefully and see if it can move. What is the peculiar structure on the under side of the body? The moth which comes from this in the spring is very large. It is covered with white and black scales and hairs which give it a mottled appearance. Examine on the under side of the head for a peculiar structure like a watch spring. This is the sucking tube used in drawing up nectar from deep tubular blossoms. When the moths are sipping nectar from "jimson weed" blossoms they can be killed by pouring a little poison down into the blossoms.

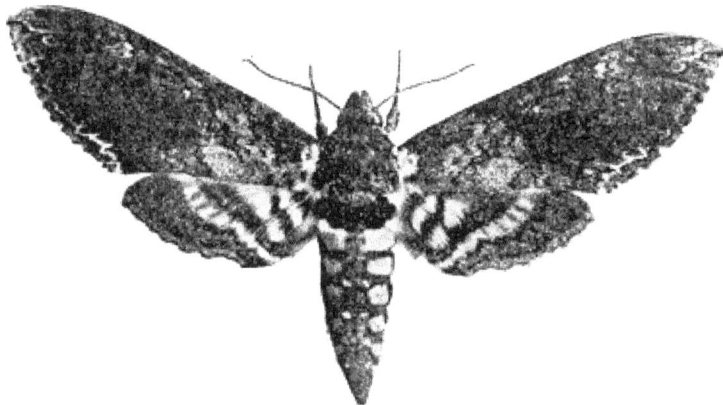

Tomato worm moth natural size.

CHAPTER IX

THE FIREFLY

THIS insect is of little economic importance to us at present but its peculiar habit of producing light makes it a very striking form and one which deserves study. The firefly is a beetle, and begins to make its appearance the latter part of June when the darkest nights may be one solid glow of fire. They live largely in damp places and bottoms at night are specked with their tiny flashes of light. The larval or grub stage is passed on the ground beneath grass, weeds and rubbish where they often prey upon other insects. In some cases the grubs may be able to produce light though as a rule the luminous grub-like creature or glow-worm is a wingless adult firefly.

OBSERVATIONS AND STUDIES

Firefly beetles on sour-dock leaf.

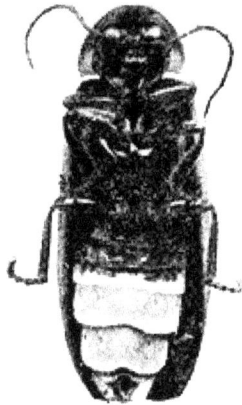

Lower surface of firefly beetle enlarged to show the light producing segments of the abdomen.

Watch for the first appearance of the fireflies in the evening and see where they come from. Do they all appear at once or only a few at first? Do they fly fast? How often is the light produced? Will they produce the light while on the ground? When they fly do they stay near the ground or high in the air? Do they light in trees?

Catch one of the fireflies in your hat and examine it carefully. How large is it? Describe briefly its size, shape and color. Are its wing covers hard like other beetles? Where is the light produced? What color is the light? Is it bright? Hold the firefly on the opposite side of a sheet of paper and see if the light will show through. Try the same with your hat, coat sleeve and other objects. This light is extremely penetrating and unlike the light of a lamp is produced with the generation of very little heat. Will it continue to flash while you hold it? Are the segments from which the light comes the same color as the other segments of the body? Crush the tip of the body between your thumb and finger and see if the light continues to appear. How long does it last? Collect a number of the fireflies and put them in a bottle and see if the light is strong enough to enable you to read.

The firefly has proven to us that our methods of producing light are extremely wasteful since much of the energy is lost in heat and it is possible that through the lesson of the firefly we may some day be able to produce better light at less expense.

CHAPTER X

THE WHITE GRUB OR JUNE-BUG

White grub feeding on roots of corn plant, enlarged.

THIS insect is more familiar to country children in the grub stage. Every one who has followed a plow in rich sod land has seen these fat, white coiled grubs roll down into the furrow when the plow turns them up. They are in the ground feeding on the roots of plants. Often all the roots of grass in lawns and meadows are eaten off and the sod dies and can be rolled up like strips of carpet. This insect breeds largely in sod and when this is plowed under and other crops are planted the grubs may injure them severely. Corn, wheat, oats and truck crops are severely injured. In some cases the grubs may feed for three years before they change to the pupa and later to the adult beetle. To control this pest, plow in the fall and rotate crops, so that sod will not remain on the same land too long.

June beetle showing stages of development. The larva or grub worm is feeding on roots under ground; the pupa and adult are shown above ground.

The beetles come from the ground or may be plowed out in May and June and are commonly spoken of as May-beetles or June-bugs. They are usually of a yellowish-brown color and are often troublesome coming into the house at night where they buzz about the light, bumping into everything until they finally drop heavily to the floor. All country boys and girls know these beetles.

Observations and Studies

Collect a number of the grubs from the ground and examine them for legs, eyes and mouth. How many legs have they? Can you find eyes? What use would they have for eyes while in the ground? Do they bite? Place them on the table and see how they move. What color are they? Do you find spines or hair on their bodies? Pull up a little grass by the roots and put it in a jelly tumbler with soil and put some of the grubs in with it. Water it so as to keep it growing and follow the development of the grubs.

Collect some of the beetles and put them in a bottle and watch them crawl about. Where are their wings? How can they get them out when they want to fly? How many legs have they? Examine the tip of the feet for hooks. What are these used for? Can they chew leaves? Where are their eyes? Do you find feelers and if so where?

Write a short description of the grub and the beetle and make careful drawings of them.

CHAPTER XI

THE COLORADO POTATO BEETLE

The Colorado potato beetle showing stages of development and work on a potato plant. Note the small patch of eggs and different sized grub on the plant and the grub, pupa and adult at side.

THIS is one of the worst pests of the potato. As the name would imply it came originally from Colorado but is common now all over the country. The full grown insect is short and thick with a hard shell, striped with yellow and black. The grubs, on the other hand, are soft and red or orange with black spots. Both the grubs and the beetles feed on potatoes and often completely strip them of their leaves. Since they feed on foliage they can be very quickly destroyed by dusting or spraying the plants with a poison such as Paris green or arsenate of lead. The patches of yellow or reddish eggs are found mostly on the under side of the potato leaves. When the fat grubs are full-fed they go into the ground and change to pupae and later to the striped beetles. This pest should not be mistaken for the so-called old-fashioned potato beetles which are long and slender and either bluish grey in color or striped with yellow and black. These are blister beetles and are entirely different.

OBSERVATIONS AND STUDIES

Watch for the first appearance of the adult beetles in the spring when the potatoes are just beginning to come up. They pass the winter under ground and in the spring come out ready to lay eggs on the young potatoes. Collect and examine the adults. How many stripes have they? Collect packets of eggs and count them. How many eggs in most packets? How are they attached to the leaf? How large are the grubs when they hatch from the egg? Examine the grubs where they are feeding on potatoes. Do they eat holes through the leaf, or do they eat away the entire leaf? How fast do they grow? Collect a few in a glass tumbler. Feed them and watch them grow. What do they do when you touch them? What does the hard backed beetle do when it is touched? Collect some of the large grubs with tightly stuffed bodies and put them in a jar with dirt or sand and see where they go. After a week dig them out and see what they look like.

Write a short description of the eggs, grubs and beetle, its work and means of killing it when it is feeding on potatoes. Make careful drawings of a cluster of eggs, the grub and the beetle.

CHAPTER XII

THE LADY-BEETLE

"Hurt no living thing:
Ladybird, nor butterfly,
Nor moth with dusty wing,
Nor cricket chirping cheerily,
Nor grasshopper so light of leap,
Nor dancing gnat, nor beetle fat,
Nor harmless worms that creep."

—CHRISTINA ROSSETTI.

THE lady-beetles comprise one family of small beetles, which is famous for the number of beneficial forms it includes. With but two exceptions the American forms feed upon other insects, in most cases pests such as plant-lice and scale insects. From the time they hatch from the egg until they pupate and again after the beetle stage is reached they are regular tigers after plant-lice. They catch and hold their prey between the front feet while they devour it bodily. The larva of the lady-beetle has an astonishing capacity for in one day it will eat several times its own weight of plant-lice. Farmers and fruit growers could hardly get along without the help of these small beetles and yet unfortunately thousands are often destroyed by those who do not know of their beneficial work.

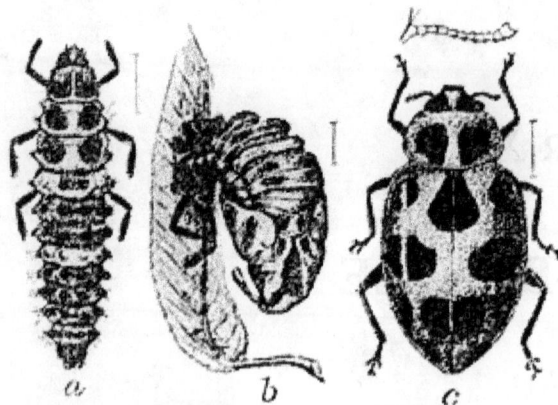

The spotted lady-beetle; a, larva; b, pupa; c, adult; enlarged. (After Chittenden, U. S. Dept. Agri.)

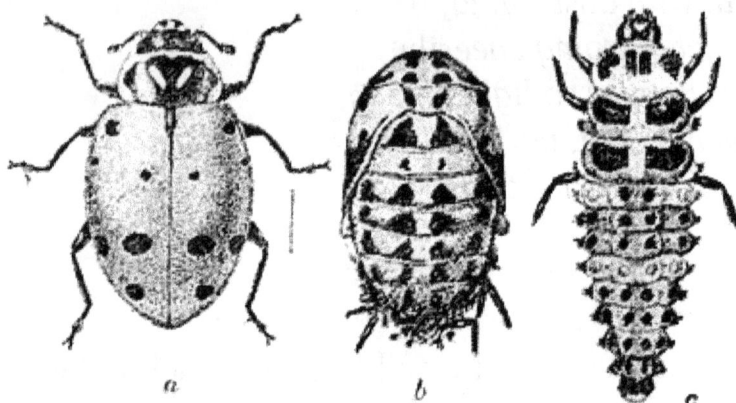

The convergent lady-beetle; a, adult; b, pupa; c, larva; all enlarged. (After Chittenden, U. S. Dept. Agri.)

The lady-beetles, or lady-birds as they are often called, are fairly uniform in shape and color. They are oval or round in outline with the back rounded or elevated and the underside flat. In color they are usually either orange or yellow, checkered or blotched with black or black with yellow or bright orange markings. They closely resemble small tortoises. Unfortunately several plant feeding beetles are similar in shape and color which casts reflections on the lady-beetles.

The grub of the lady-beetle is usually black or dull colored with red or yellow markings which make it very conspicuous. It runs about over foliage and is broad in front and tapers to a point behind. When the grub is full fed it attaches the top of its body to a leaf, twig or other object and pupates. In the pupal stage it is often protected with spines and is able to lift the front end of the body up and down when disturbed, producing a light tapping sound.

The lady-beetle usually hides in rubbish about the base of trees or in some cases even enter homes for the winter months, coming out with the spring to deposit small masses of oval yellow or orange eggs on plants infested with lice. They breed rapidly and with the help of parasites and other beneficial insects usually control the plant-lice pests.

OBSERVATIONS AND STUDIES

Examine about fruit trees, shade trees, truck crops and in wheat fields for the brightly marked beetles. Watch them move about the plant in search of food. Can they fly? Do you find them eating the leaves? Do you find any green lice near them? See if they feed on these lice. Examine also for the soft bodied, tiger-like grubs. Do they eat the lice? Do they travel fast? Have they wings? See if you can find any of the pupae attached to limbs or twigs and if so, tickle them with a straw or a pencil and see them "bow." Keep a record of the different trees and plants on which you find lady-beetles.

Collect several of the beetles and the grubs and keep them in a bottle or jelly glass. Leave them without food for a day and then give them some green plant-lice and watch them devour the lice. How many lice can one eat in a day? How do they go about devouring a louse? Do they simply suck out the blood, or is the louse completely devoured? Supposing that for each apple tree in Missouri there are one hundred lady-beetles and that each beetle devours fifteen lice in a day, does it not seem worth while protecting them and encouraging such work? A little time spent in acquainting one's self with the good work of such forms as these will help greatly in the fight on our insect foes. Make drawings of and describe briefly the different stages of the lady-beetles.

Chapter XIII

THE DRAGON-FLY

Cast off skin of dragon-fly nymph, showing shape and position taken on a twig when the adult winged form emerged from the last nymph stage.

WHAT child is there that is not familiar with the insect commonly known as the dragon-fly, snake doctor or snake feeder? Every lover of the stream or pond has seen these miniature aeroplanes darting now here, now there but ever retracing their airy flight along the water's edge or dipping in a sudden nose dive to skim its very surface. At times it is seen to rest lazily, wings out-stretched, perched on some projecting reed or other object. But when approached how suddenly it "takes off" and is out of reach. The dragon-fly is an almost perfect model of the modern monoplane. Its two long wings on either side are the planes, its head the nose, its thorax the fuselage and its long projecting abdomen the tail or rudder. On wing the dragon-fly is one of the swiftest and most powerful insects. The dragon-flies are found all over the world being most abundant in the warmer regions where rainfall and bodies of water are abundant. For breeding they require water, their immature stages living under water feeding on aquatic animal life. Our present order of dragon-flies is the remains of an ancient race of insects of immense size. From fossil remains we learn that ancient dragon-flies had a wing expanse of three feet.

The dragon-fly is a beneficial insect thruout life. The young feed on mosquito wigglers and similar life in ponds and streams while the adults dart here and there over ponds, fields or lawn catching mosquitoes and other winged insects. Many look upon the dragon-fly as a dangerous stinging insect but it is entirely harmless and can be handled without the least danger. They vary greatly in size and appearance. The so-called damsel-flies form a group of dragon-flies or Odonata which rest with the wings in a vertical position and the young aquatic stages are more slender.

In color markings dragon-flies include all hues of the rainbow tho as a rule they do not have such extravagant colors as the butterflies.

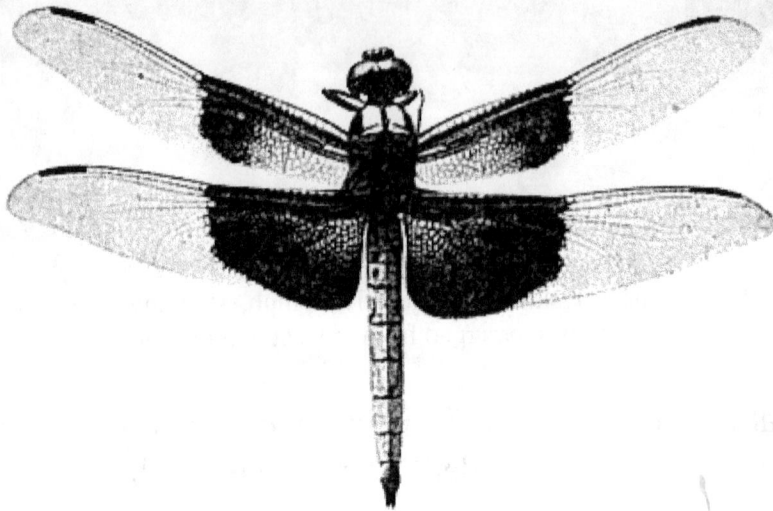

One of our common dragon-flies found about ponds and streams.

Observations and Field Studies

Go into the fields and study and collect the different kinds of dragon-flies and their young stages from the bottoms of ponds. How swiftly can they fly? Do they fly high in the air as well as near the water or surface of the earth? Can you see them catch other insects? Do birds catch them and eat them? Take a position along the edge of a pond and as they come flying by swing swiftly with your net and catch one. Examine it carefully. Note the strength of the long, slender wings with their lace-like network of veins. Measure the distance across the back from tip to tip of wings. Compare this with the length from tip of head to the tip of the abdomen. Examine the head with its large compound eyes and the chewing mouth parts. Note the strong thorax which is filled with muscles to operate the wings in flight. How many segments are there to the abdomen?

With the hands or with a bucket dip up a quantity of mud and trash from the bottom of a pond and pile it on the bank. As the water soaks away watch for signs of life in the mass. If you find a few small creatures, say half an inch long with large head and eyes, broad body and with six rather long legs they are probably the nymph stages of dragon-flies. Wash the mud off of them so that you can examine them carefully. With a straw probe in the mouth and you will find that the lower lip is a long elbowed structure which can be suddenly thrown out in front of it and with a pair of pincher-like prongs at the tip it can catch and hold its prey. Some forms keep their bodies covered with mud so that they can slowly creep up close to their prey.

Collect several nymphs and keep them in a jar of water and study their movements and feeding habits. Disturb one with a pencil or straw and see how it darts forward. It has a water chamber in the large intestines, including also the respiratory tracheal gills, from which the water can be suddenly squirted which throws the insect forward. The escaping stream of water forces the insect forward on the same principle as the rotating lawn sprinkler. If you collect some almost mature nymphs and keep them for a time in a vessel of water you may see them crawl out of the water, shed their skin and change to winged adults. Collect a few adults of different species for pinning in your permanent collection.

CHAPTER XIV

THE SQUASH BUG

THIS common blackish or earth-colored bug is usually called the squash stink-bug. It has a very disagreeable odor which gives it this name. When disturbed it throws off from scent glands a small quantity of an oily substance which produces this odor. This is a protection to it for few birds or animals care to feed on it. Most species of sap or blood sucking true bugs have a similar protecting odor.

Pumpkin in field covered with adults and nymphs of squash stink-bug.

The squash bug feeds largely on squash and pumpkins. It has a slender beak with needle-like mouth parts which are stuck into the plant for extracting the sap. It feeds only on plant sap. When it can not get squash or pumpkins it will feed on watermelons, muskmelons and related crops. It is very destructive to these crops. It not only extracts sap thus weakening the plant but it also seems to poison the plant while feeding. In this way its bite injures the plant something like the effects of the bed-bug's bite on our flesh. It feeds first on the leaves and vines often killing them in a few days. Later it may cluster and feed on the unripe squashes or pumpkins in such numbers as to completely cover them. Every country boy or girl has seen these stinking bugs on pumpkins in the corn field, at corn cutting time in the fall.

Cluster of golden-brown eggs of squash stink-bug showing two recently hatched nymphs.

The squash bug lives thru the winter as the matured winged insect. It flies from its food plant to winter quarters late in the fall. For winter protection it may enter buildings, hide under shingles on roofs, crawl into piles of lumber, under bark of dead trees or stumps or hide under any similar protection. When its chosen food crops begin to come up in the spring it leaves its winter home and flies in search of food. After feeding for a time the female lays patches of oval, flattened, gold-colored eggs set on edge. When first deposited the eggs have a pale color but in a short time the golden color appears. In some cases only three or four eggs may be found in one patch while again there may be twenty or thirty of them. They are so brightly colored that they can easily be seen and most boys and girls have seen them on the leaves of squashes or pumpkins.

In a few days after they are laid they hatch and out of each crawls a small, long-legged blackish or greenish young bug called the nymph. These little fellows usually stay in a crowd hiding on the under side of a leaf. After feeding for a time their leaf begins to turn yellow and soon dies. Then they move to a new leaf. As they feed they grow rapidly and after shedding their skins they change to the second nymph stage. This shedding of their skins or molting occurs five times before they mature. Of course each time before the old skin or suit of clothes is discarded a new one is developed beneath. The females may continue to deposit eggs for later clusters of young. They become most abundant on the crop late in the fall. Just before cold weather sets in the adults again seek winter shelter.

This is a very difficult insect to control. Since it feeds on liquid sap only it is impossible to kill it by spraying the crop with a poison such as arsenate of lead. It can not chew and swallow such poison. The young can be killed fairly well with a spray or dust containing nicotine but such treatments are not effective against the adults or nearly mature nymphs. A better method is to destroy all the bugs possible in the fall before they go to the winter protection and then watch for and destroy the adults and the eggs masses in the spring when they appear on the young crop. If the first adults and the eggs and newly hatched nymphs are destroyed the crop can be protected against the destructive work later.

OBSERVATIONS AND FIELD STUDIES

Squash stink-bug adult and nymph extracting sap from squash.

Plant a few squash hills in the garden in the spring and also plant a few seeds in rich dirt in discarded tin cans or flower pots. As the spring advances and the squashes start to vine watch for squash bugs on them.

Examine in piles of lumber, stove wood and under bark for some of the bugs before they come to the squash hills. If any are found put them on the squash plants in flower pots and cover them with a pint mason fruit jar. Watch for eggs to appear on the plants and also examine for eggs on the squashes in the garden. When eggs appear examine them carefully, measure them and write a brief description of them. Try to mash them between your fingers. When they hatch carefully study the young nymph and describe it. Can you see the slender beak which incloses the mouth parts? How many joints are there to the antennae? As the nymph grows watch it shed its skin. How does it do it? Where does its skin first crack? Save the cast skin and try to follow the nymph thru all the nymph stages to the adult. Collect a bottle of the nymphs of varying sizes from the garden. Examine them and describe the different stages. Can you see the wings forming on the backs of the older nymphs? How many small wing pads are there? Examine the adult closely and write a careful description of it. Can you find where the secretion that causes the odor is produced? How long will the odor stay on your hands? Can you wash it off? Spread the wings of the adult and make a careful drawing of one front and one hind wing showing accurately the wing veins. In the garden try to protect all the hills of squash from the bugs except one or two used for your studies. Write a brief description of your methods of control.

CHAPTER XV

THE PLANT-LOUSE

FOR this chapter any common species of plant-louse may be used. If the study is made in the spring the louse on rose, apple, clover, wheat or any other crop may be used. If the study is made in the fall the species on turnips, corn or other plant or crop may be selected. The different species vary greatly but for these studies any available species will be satisfactory.

Black winter eggs of Aphis showing how they are deposited in masses on twigs of apple. (After U. S. Dept. Agri.)

The plant-louse or aphis is a sap-sucking insect which feeds and multiplies rapidly often seriously injuring crops. The loss of sap together with the poisoning effect of the bite causes the weakening of the plant or leaf with its ultimate death if feeding continues. The greatest damage is usually done during cold springs or during a cool rainy period. This prevents the enemies of the louse from increasing and attacking it while the weather may not be too severe to prevent the louse from working. Under favorable climatic conditions the natural enemies of the louse as a rule are able to hold it in check. The principal enemies of the louse are certain small insect feeding birds, lady-beetles, syrphid-flies, lace-wings and tiny wasp parasites. The beneficial work of the lady-beetles is discussed in an earlier chapter. The birds and lady-beetles devour them bodily, the larvæ of the lace-wings and syrphid-flies extract their blood while the wasps live as internal parasites.

In the latitude of Missouri the plant-lice as a rule live thru the winter in the form of a fertile egg attached to the twigs of trees and shrubs. The winter egg is produced by a true female plant-louse. As a rule there is only one generation of true males and females produced each year. This brood develops late in the fall to produce the fertilized winter eggs. In the spring these eggs hatch and the tiny nymphs begin to extract sap. On maturing they begin to give birth to young lice. Throughout the summer this method of reproduction continues. These summer forms are known as the stem mothers or agamic females. These are not true females for they produce living young in place of eggs and during the summer no male lice are produced at all. This is nature's way of increasing the race of plant-lice rapidly. Late in the fall again a brood of true males and females is produced. During the summer the plant-lice increase more rapidly than any other type of insect.

Plant-lice vary in size, color and general appearance. Many are green while some are red or black or covered with a cottony secretion.

OBSERVATIONS AND FIELD STUDIES

Plant some melon, radish or other seeds in fertile soil in pots for use in this study. When lice appear on crops in the garden or field, collect a leaf with a few on it and carefully transfer them to the leaves on your potted plants. Watch the lice feed and increase from day to day. A reading lens or a magnifying glass will be helpful as plant-lice are very small. How do they move about? Can you count their legs? How many have they? Can you see their eyes and feelers? When feeding observe how the beak is pressed against the leaf. Disturb one while it is feeding and see it attempt to loosen its mouth parts.

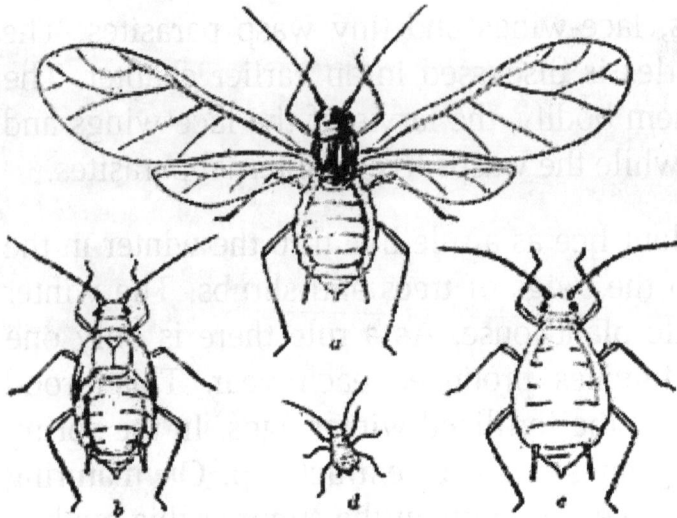

Common apple aphis showing a winged and wingless agamic summer forms at a and c, one with wing pads formed at b, and a recently born young at d. (After U. S. Dept. Agri.)

In the garden examine and see if you can find lady-beetles or other parasites attacking the lice. Collect some of the enemies of the lice for your collection. Make a gallon of tobacco tea by soaking one pound of tobacco stems or waste tobacco in one gallon of water for a day or use one ounce of forty per cent nicotine sulphate in three gallons of soap suds and spray or sprinkle infested bushes or vegetables with it. In an hour examine and see what effect it has had on the plant-lice. Nicotine is the most effective chemical for killing plant-lice. Do any of the lice develop wings? If so, how many? Wings develop on some of the lice at times when a plant or crop becomes too heavily infested by them. This enables some of the lice to spread to new food plants before old plants are completely destroyed and the colony of lice starved.

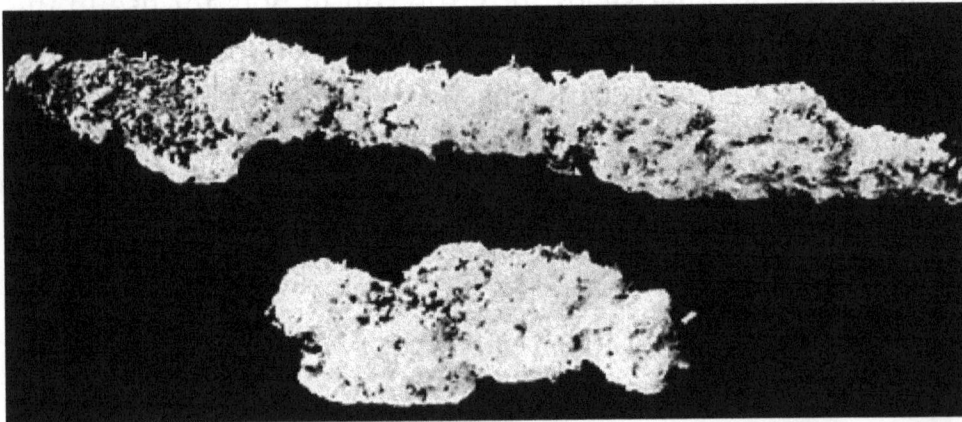

Wooly apple aphis, showing how they cluster in masses on limbs and secrete the white, wooly protection over their bodies.

Make a careful enlarged drawing of a winged plant-louse and a wingless one showing legs, feelers, beak, honey dew tubes on back and body segmentation. If ants are seen to attend the lice observe them carefully and describe their work. The ants feed on a sweet honey dew excretion discharged by the lice.

CHAPTER XVI

THE HONEY BEE

"Simple and sweet is their food; they eat no flesh of the living."

—VON KUEBEL.

ONE can hardly believe that this small, ever busy creature each year gathers many million dollars worth of products for man in this country alone to say nothing of its inestimable value on the farm and especially in the orchard, where it assists in carrying pollen from blossom to blossom. It is of far greater value to man as a carrier of pollen than it is as a honey gatherer and yet under especially favorable conditions in one year a strong colony may produce between twenty-five and thirty dollars worth of honey.

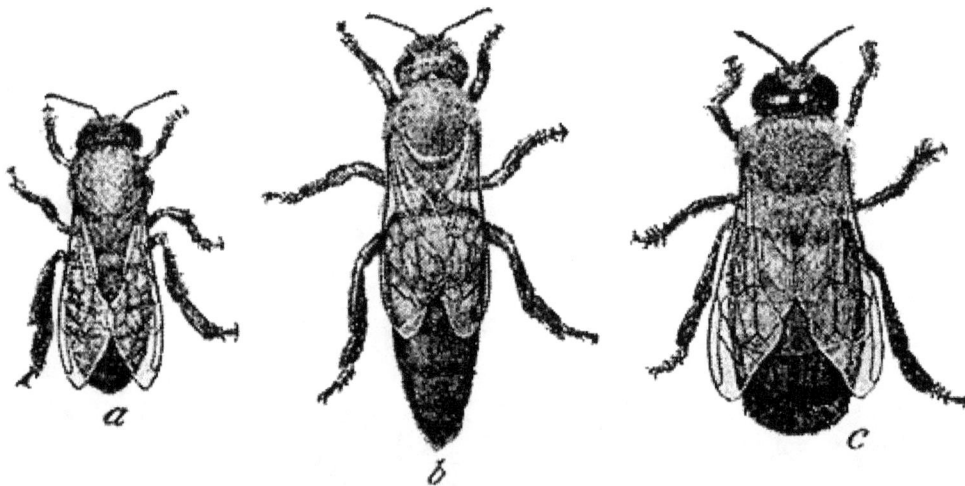

Worker, queen and drone honey bees; all about natural size. (After Phillips, U. S. Dept. of Agri.)

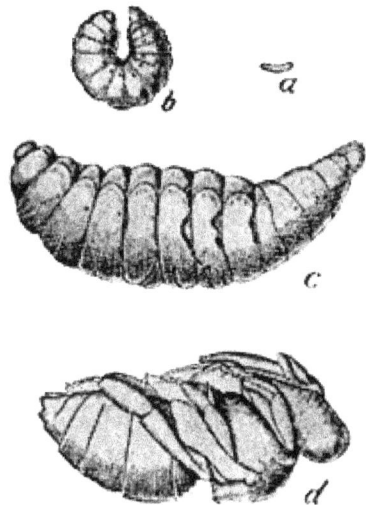

Stages of development of honey bee; a, egg; b, young grub; c, full-fed grub; d, pupa; all enlarged. (After Phillips, U. S. Dept. Agri.)

The general habits of the bee are fairly well known by all. They live in colonies consisting largely of workers, one female or queen and males or drones. Whenever the number of workers becomes sufficiently large to warrant a division of the colony, a young queen is reared by the workers and just before she matures, the old queen leaves with about half of the workers to establish a new colony. This division of the colony is called swarming. If a hive, box or other acceptable home is not provided soon after the swarm comes out and clusters, it may fly to the woods and establishes itself in a hollow tree where the regular work of honey gathering is continued. This accounts for so many bee-trees in the woods. The bee has been handled by man for ages, but it readily becomes wild when allowed to escape to the woods.

The bee colony offers one of the best examples to show what can be accomplished by united effort where harmony prevails. Certain of the workers gather honey, others are nurses for the queen and young brood in the hive, others guard the hive and repel intruders, and others care for the hive by mending breaks and providing new comb as it is needed. Each knows its work and goes about it without interfering with the work of others. It is one huge assemblage of individuals under one roof where harmony and industry prevail.

Throughout the long, hot summer days the workers are busy from daylight until dark gathering nectar, while at night they force currents of air thru the hive to evaporate the excess water from the nectar. When flowers are not available near the hive they simply fly until they find them, be it one, two or more miles. As long as they are able to gather honey they continue to do so and when they give out they drop in the field and are forgotten, others rushing to take their place. Often when winter is approaching and the store of honey is low the less vigorous ones are cast out from the hive and left to die. If man could learn a few of the lessons which the bee teaches, he would be a better, a more useful and a wiser addition to society.

OBSERVATIONS AND STUDIES

Two colonies of bees poorly cared for. Note box hives, crowding, lack of shade, and high weeds. It is a crime to treat bees this way.

Go into the fields and study the work of the bee. Follow it from flower to flower. See if it visits different kinds of flowers or if it gathers its whole load of honey from one kind. Make a list of all the blossoms you find bees visiting. Does the bee move slowly from flower to flower? Can you see it thrust its tongue into the flower? How long does it stay on one blossom? Does it visit red clover? Pull a red clover blossom apart and compare the depth of the blossom with the length of the honey bee's tongue, and determine the reason why it does not visit red clover. The bumble-bee has a much longer tongue so it can get the nectar from red clover blossoms. Without the bumble-bee clover seed could not be successfully grown. Can you see small balls of yellow pollen on the hind legs of the bee? The pollen is collected from blossoms and is pasted on to the outside of the hind legs in the pollen basket. When the bee returns to the hive, it stores the small balls of pollen in the cells of the comb for use later in the preparation of bee-bread. When the bee is disturbed in the field does it fly away or will it sting? When it stings does it always lose its sting? What makes the sting of the bee poisonous? Examine the wings of bees in the field and note how they are torn from continued work of gathering honey. The older ones often lose so much of their wings, that they can no longer carry loads of honey. Where is the honey carried and how is it placed in the honey cells in the hive?

A strong colony of bees properly housed and shaded. This colony in a very unfavorable season stored about 50 pounds of surplus honey.

Go now to a hive and study the bees as they go and come. Do those returning fly as fast as those which leave? Why not? When they return do they come direct to the mouth of the hive? Do those which leave fly direct from the hive or circle about first? Can you detect guards which move about at the entrance of the hive? What happens when a fly or other insect alights near the opening? Will the bees sting when you disturb them about the hive? If possible study the colony inside the hive. To do this you will need smoke to subdue the guards and a veil to protect the face. Can you find the queen? Is she larger than the workers? Examine for honey-comb, bee-bread, worker brood, queen cells and drone cells. If possible study the actions of a colony while swarming.

Write a brief report of what you can learn of the life, work and habits of the honey bee.

_____

"Happy insect, what can be
*   In happiness compared to thee?*
Fed with nourishment divine,
*   The dewy morning's gentle wine!*

"Nature waits upon thee still,
*   And thy verdant cup does fill;*
'Tis filled wherever thou doest tread
*   Nature's self thy Ganymede.*

"Thou doest drink and dance and sing,
*   Happier than the happiest king!*
All the fields which thou doest see,
*   All the plants belong to thee,*
All the summer hours produce,
*   Fertile made with early juice,*
Man for thee does sow and plough,
*   Farmer he, and landlord thou."*

—From THE GREEK OF ANACREON.

CHAPTER XVII

THE ANT

THE ants are closely related to the bees and are similar to them in many respects. They live in colonies consisting of workers, drones, and a queen. The males or drones appear at swarming time and the workers are divided into various castes—warriors, guards, nurses, etc. Those families of ants, however, which seem to have what approaches real intelligence, far outstrip the bees in many respects. In some cases ants seem to be able to plan and carry out lines of work very much the same as man does. The various stages of human intelligence or races of men from the savage to the intelligent man are in a way similar to the various races of ants. There are ants which live as hunters, others which live as shepherds and still others more highly developed which grow crops either in or near the nest as is the case with the fungus growing ants. This striking similarity between the development of ants and man offers ground for much speculation.

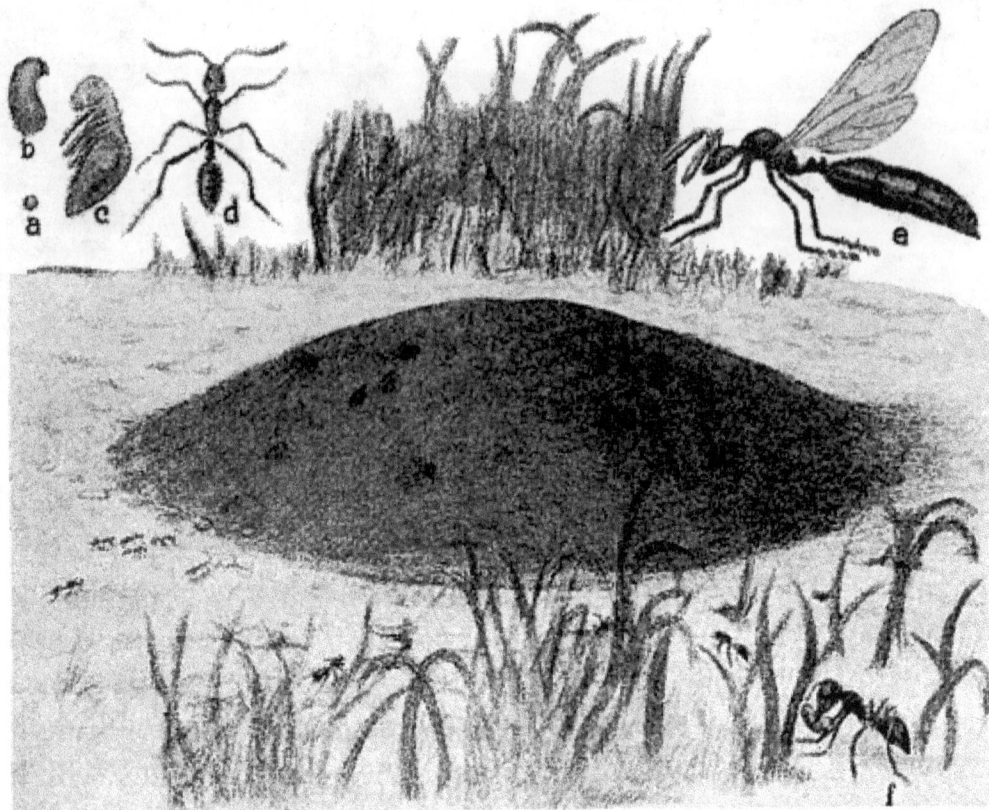

Ant hill showing activity and stages of development; a, egg; b, young grub; c, pupa; d, worker; e, queen with wings; f, worker carrying young grub; all enlarged. The ant hill and workers at work much reduced.

Some ants may be of considerable value to man while others are the source of great annoyance and injury. The tidy housewife usually places the ant in the same category with cockroaches and bed-bugs and the corn growers attribute much of the injury to young corn to the work of the small cornfield ant which acts as a shepherd of the corn root-louse. Ants are usually more destructive by protecting and caring for other pests than by attacking the crop direct.

Every country child is familiar with ants. They are met every day during the summer, scampering across paths, tugging at some unfortunate insect, or sticking to one's tongue when he eats berries. Ants are as numerous as the stars in the skies and vary in size. They are found from the tropics to the frozen north, in deserts, swamps and in fact, almost any place where plants or animals live. They do not waste time building or manufacturing a complicated nest like wasps and bees, so when food is scare, or for other reasons they need to move they simply "pack up" and migrate. This, together with the fact that they feed on almost every imaginable kind of plant and animal material, accounts in part for the fact that they are the rulers of the insect world.

STUDIES AND OBSERVATIONS

It is easy to study the out-door life of ants, but it is most difficult to follow their activities in the nest. Go into the field or out on the school grounds and watch along paths or bare spots for ants. Soon red or black fellows will be seen hurrying along after food; ants are always in a hurry when they are after food. Follow them and watch them catch and carry home small insects. If they do not find worms or other small insects, drop a small caterpillar near one of them and see what happens. Can they drag away a caterpillar as large as themselves? Some of them may be after honey dew, fruit juice or other material of this nature and they should be observed collecting it. Ants collect about plants or shrubs which are overrun with green lice, and feed on a sweet liquid which the lice produce. Watch them collect the honey dew from the lice. Do they injure the lice? Can you see the two short tubes on the back of the louse?

Locate an ant nest or hill. Observe the workers carrying out small pellets of earth or gravels. Is the earth they bring out the same color as the surface soil? How deep may they go to get it? Do they move about as if they were in a hurry? Who sends them out with the earth? Why do they bring it out? Is it dropped as soon as the ant comes out of the hole or is it carried some distance? The small ant found along paths usually makes a small ridge all the way around the entrance. While some of the ants are making the nest, others are collecting food. Watch for some of these and see what they bring. Do they stop to eat before going down into the nest? Dig into a large ant hill and see what can be found. Describe briefly what is found. Do you find any small soft grubs and oval cocoons? These are the young ants and they are perfectly helpless and must be fed, bathed and cared for by the workers or nurses. The workers pick these up between their pinchers and carry them away when the nest is disturbed. Do the workers fight to protect the nest? Collect some of the workers which are carrying away the young and keep them in a jar with bits of bark and see what they do with the young.

Describe briefly what you are able to find out about ant life and behavior; also make drawings of an ant, the young and a nest.

"A pensy ant, right trig and clean,
Came ae day whidding o'er the green,
Where, to advance her pride, she saw
A Caterpillar, moving slaw.
'Good ev'n t' ye, Mistress Ant,' said he;
'How's a' at home? I'm blyth to s' ye!'
The saucy ant view'd him wi' scorn,
Nor wad civilities return;
But gecking up her head, quoth she,
'Poor animal! I pity thee;
Wha scarce can claim to be a creature,
But some experiment O' Nature,
Whase silly shape displeased her eye,
And thus unfinished was flung bye.
For me, I'm made wi' better grace,
Wi' active limbs and lively face;
And cleverely can move wi' ease
Frae place to place where'er I please;
Can foot a minuet or jig,
And snoov't like ony whirly-gig;
Which gars my jo aft grip my hand,
Till his heart pitty-pattys, and—
But laigh my qualities I bring,
To stand up clashing wi' a thing,
A creeping thing the like o' thee,
Not worthy o' a farewell to' ye!'
The airy Ant syne turned awa,
And left him wi' a proud gaffa.

"The Caterpillar was struck dumb,
And never answered her a mum:
The humble reptile fand some pain,

Thus to be bantered wi' disdain.
But tent neist time the Ant came by,
The worm was grown a Butterfly;
Transparent were his wings and fair,
Which bare him flight'ring through the air.
Upon a flower he stapt his flight,
And thinking on his former slight,
Thus to the Ant himself addrest:
'Pray, Madam, will ye please to rest?
And notice what I now advise:
Inferiors ne'er too much despise,
For fortune may gie sic a turn,
To raise aboon ye what ye scorn:
For instance, now I spread my wing
In air, while you're a creeping thing!'"

—ALLAN RAMSAY.

www.ingramcontent.com/pod-product-compliance
Lightning Source LLC
Chambersburg PA
CBHW080526030426

42337CB00023B/4640